Military Memoirs

of

Four Brothers

Engaged in the Service
of their Country,
as well in the
New World and Africa
as on the
Continent of Europe

MILITARY MEMOIRS

OF

FOUR BROTHERS

ENGAGED IN THE SERVICE
OF THEIR COUNTRY,
AS WELL IN THE
NEW WORLD AND AFRICA
AS ON THE
CONTINENT OF EUROPE

BY

THE SURVIVOR
(THOMAS FERNYHOUGH)

The Spellmount Library of Military History

SPELLMOUNT
Staplehurst

British Library Cataloguing in Publication Data:
A catalogue record for this book is available
from the British Library

Copyright © Spellmount Ltd 2002
Introduction © Philip J Haythornthwaite 2002

ISBN 1-86227-127-5

First published in 1829

This edition first published in the UK in 2002
in
The Spellmount Library of Military History
by
Spellmount Limited
The Old Rectory
Staplehurst
Kent TN12 0AZ
United Kingdom

Tel: 01580 893730
Fax: 01580 893731
E-mail: enquiries@spellmount.com
Website: www.spellmount.com

1 3 5 7 9 8 6 4 2

Printed in Great Britain by
T.J. International Ltd
Padstow, Cornwall

AN INTRODUCTION
By Philip J. Haythornthwaite

Military Memoirs of Four Brothers is one of the rarer personal accounts of the Napoleonic Wars and is somewhat unusual in being composed primarily of the journals and letters of two brothers, involving both maritime and land operations. It was published in 1829, with a second edition in the following year; a third edition, of 1838, was limited to 30 copies printed for the author's friends. Like some other contemporary memoirs, it was published anonymously, with some personalities being identified only by initials.

The author of the book was Captain Thomas Fernyhough (1777–1844), one of the 'Four Brothers', the eldest son of John Fernyhough of Lichfield, Staffordshire (1745–1835) and his wife, Sarah (née Thorneloe, 1749–1828). John Fernyhough had six sons: Thomas, John, Henry and Robert, with whom the book is concerned; William (1788–1805), Charles (who died shortly after birth in 1783) and two daughters, Anna (1775–1803) and Sarah (1792–1835). William, the brother who did not follow a military career, was an artist and architect, and upon his death at Chester on 16 January 1805, was described as a 'drawing-master; a modest and ingenious young man'.[1] The family was probably typical of the middle class and minor gentry which produced a large proportion of the nation's military and naval officers, and even the father of the Four Brothers, John Fernyhough, served in the Staffordshire Yeomanry during this period of threat from French invasion.

Much of the author's military career is outlined in the book. Born on 20 May 1777, Thomas Fernyhough was commissioned as an ensign upon the augmentation of the militia in 1797. In addition to his period of service in the regular army, he was most associated with the militia of his own county. The Staffordshire Militia (which was granted the title 'King's Own' in 1805) was embodied for full-time service from 1793 until April 1801, from March 1803 until 1814, and again in 1815 until April 1816. It was as a lieutenant in the Staffordshire Militia that Thomas was a witness to the execution of two members of the York Hussars (one of the many units of the British Army at the period which were recruited from foreigners), on Bincombe Down, near Weymouth, on 30 June 1801. The case was one of some notoriety at the time (and was later recorded in a short story by Thomas Hardy), and from its prominence in his book, clearly made a great impression upon the young officer. The purpose of the solemn and awful ceremony of execution was to convey such an impression, and to deliver a warning, to the spectators, for which purpose all the troops in the area were assembled: the 2nd Dragoons (Royal Scots Greys), Rifle Corps, and the militias of Staffordshire, Berkshire and North Devon.

Shortly after, Thomas Fernyhough transferred to the regular army, by obtaining a commission in the 60th (Royal American) Regiment. Raised in 1755 for service in the Americas, the regiment was unique in the regular army as being the receptacle for foreign recruits; at the time he joined, it was receiving drafts of men from a number of 'foreign corps' which were then being disbanded. (In his list of these units, Thomas mentions the Chasseurs Britanniques, a corps which actually remained independent, and he uses a phonetic spelling 'Levenstein' for units which bore the name 'Löwenstein'). His career in the 60th was of short duration, however, the climate and diseases of the West Indies causing him to return to Europe, where he exchanged to half-pay retirement in the 40th Foot. Shortly after his arrival home, he lost two of his siblings: sister Anna died on 14 July 1803, and his brother Henry (born 28 May 1782), only lately appointed a 2nd lieutenant in the Royal Marines, died as the consequence of an accidental injury on 30 November 1803.

The principal part of the book concerns the careers of the remaining two brothers. Born on 7 May 1779, John Fernyhough was commissioned a 2nd lieutenant in the Portsmouth Division of Marines on 6 August 1800. The military element of the Royal Navy, whose personnel served aboard all British warships, became the Royal Marines on 29 April 1802. John was appointed to the 80-gun ship-of-the-line HMS *Donegal*, and his letters and journal tell of typical cruising in the Mediterranean and to the West Indies, involving numerous actions and threats of action. He was promoted to 1st lieutenant (in No 125 company, Portsmouth Division) on 19 January 1805. Having been sent to Gibraltar for provisions, HMS *Donegal* just missed the Battle of Trafalgar, but its consequences led to John's death.

Two days after the battle the senior surviving French naval officer at Cadiz, Captain Julien-Marie Cosmao-Kerjulien, sailed out of that port with five ships-of-the-line that had escaped Trafalgar, and five frigates and two brigs, to attempt to recover some of the French and Spanish ships captured by the British during the battle. He had little success, recovering only two (one of which was wrecked soon after), and losing three of his ships-of-the line in a storm. One of these, the Spanish 100-gunner *Rayo*, anchored off the coast, but having suffered damage during the battle, lost her masts. On 24 October she surrendered upon the approach of two British ships, HMS *Leviathan* and the newly-arrived *Donegal*. The latter put aboard a prize-crew of 107 men, including John Fernyhough. His obituary recounted what followed:

'Aged 26, Lieut. John Fernyhough, of Lichfield. He lost his life in endeavouring to preserve the lives of the crew of the *Rayo*, Spanish three-decker, which was wrecked off St. Lucar; he was put on board with a party of marines on the 24th . . .

on the 26th came on a gale from the South-West: the prize parted her cables and went on-shore off St. Lucar. Lieut. F. volunteered his services to go in an open boat to persuade the Spaniards to save the unfortunate people of the wreck; 25 men were allotted to go with him, and when they had nearly approached the beach, a heavy squall upset the boat, and 22, including the lieutenant, perished. His death is universally lamented, as he was an able and humane officer'.[2]

Born on 4 July 1784, Robert Fernyhough began his military career in the militia, and, like his brothers John and Henry, entered the Royal Marines. Relatively early in his service, while serving aboard the 64-gunner HMS *Diadem* (the flagship of Commodore Sir Home Popham), he was appointed adjutant of the battalion of seamen and marines formed to assist the army which was to capture the Cape of Good Hope. To prepare himself for service on land, he noted that he had been studying 'Dundas', the army's manual *Rules and Regulations for the Formation, Field-Exercise and Movements of His Majesty's Forces*, written by General Sir David Dundas. In the event, he saw little action on land, but on 4 March 1806 commanded the party of marines which took possession of the French frigate *Volontaire*, and released the British prisoners she had taken when capturing some British transports.

Robert's next campaign was less successful: the British expedition to South America, initiated (without sanction) by the mercurial Home Popham, was intent on facilitating the independence of the Spanish colonies, depriving Spain of revenue and opening the region to British trade. The military contingent of the operation was led by General William Beresford (later an important figure in the Peninsular War as Marshal of the Portuguese Army), but despite the capture of Buenos Ayres in

June 1806, the Spanish inhabitants of the region were hostile, and the expedition was compelled to surrender. Having decided to support the enterprise, the British government sent reinforcements, but despite Sir Samuel Auchmuty's capture on Montevideo, a renewed attack on Buenos Ayres was conducted with such ineptitude by Sir John Whitelocke that the British had to sue for peace. Robert's journal provides a graphic account of this unhappy episode and his subsequent captivity.

After further service at sea (including another unsuccessful expedition, to the Scheldt or Walcheren in 1809), Robert's concern over his health led him to transfer to the army. After much correspondence by Thomas and himself (which demonstrates how those without the ability to purchase a commission might have to elicit patronage), and thanks to the influence of Sir William Stewart, Robert obtained a position in the 95th Regiment or Rifle Corps. Stewart had been one of the founders of this unique formation, the only regiment armed exclusively with rifles, dressed in dark green, and the most proficient light troops in the army. Their specialist skirmishing skills, and the proud boast that by providing the army's advance- and rearguards, the riflemen fired the first and last shots of every action in which they were present, produced an *esprit de corps* second to none. All three battalions of the 95th served with great distinction in the Peninsular War, notably as part of the élite Light Division.

Robert was so anxious to join the 95th that he was prepared to serve as a 'volunteer' (a young man who served as a private but lived with the officers, in the hope of stepping up to a vacant commission), but joined the 3rd Battalion as an officer. On 11 June 1812 he was promoted to 1st lieutenant in the place of Donald Macpherson ('as good a soul as ever lived [who] feared nothing either in this world or the next',[3] who had been wounded at the storming of Badajoz and who had died of his injuries at

Elvas on 7 May 1812; it was only by such deadly attrition of campaign that some officers were able to advance in rank at all. Due to their prominence in action, the 95th lost many officers. Two mentioned by Robert were 'Lieutenant M-----', presumably Henry Manners, whose knee was shattered by a grapeshot at Badajoz; and Rutherford Hawkesley, to whose grave Robert made a pilgrimage. His 'most estimable private character and numerous virtues strongly endeared him to his brother officers and a large circle of friends';[4] wounded in an attack on a redoubt before Ciudad Rodrigo on 8 January 1812, he died three days later.

It was not, however, a wound in battle that interrupted Robert's career in the Peninsula, but illness. Having witnessed the aftermath of the Battle of Salamanca, he became so weak and infirm that he was unable to follow the army in its arduous retreat from Burgos, was temporarily captured by the French, and then abandoned. He survived thanks to the assistance of a loyal comrade and of Sir Alexander Gordon, Wellington's ADC, and he seems to have been shown great kindness at this time by his commanding officer, Sir Andrew Barnard, one of the best and most highly respected officers in the army. The regard felt for him by the Fernyhough family may by gauged from the fact that the book was dedicated to him.

After a period of convalescence, and an abortive attempt to transfer (with promotion) to the 7th Battalion 60th, Robert returned to the Peninsula with the 95th, but too late to see any fighting. Similarly, he missed the expedition to New Orleans; the 'Major B-----' whom he asked if he might accompany it without orders, was clearly William Balvaird, who similarly missed the fighting in America. Robert returned to mainland Europe too late for the Battle of Waterloo, but did serve in the army of occupation in France, and with his artistic inclinations commented upon the repatriation by the Allied powers of the artworks which had been appropriated by Napoleon during his conquests and deposited in the Louvre. (Men of the 95th were deployed to prevent any French resistance against the removal of such works of art; to demonstrate their resolution they removed the lock-covers from their rifles, a gesture which prevented the spectators from causing any trouble!) Demonstrating that rank was no barrier to those of like interests, it was at the Louvre that Robert discussed Raphael's *Transfiguration* with the great Austrian Field-Marshal, Karl Philipp, Prince Schwarzenberg.

As a tribute to the 95th's distinguished service, on 16 February 1816 it was taken out of the numbered sequence of regiments and titled instead The Rifle Brigade; hence the use of that name towards the end of the account of Robert's service, which concluded in Ireland. It includes the sad death of one of his brother officers from hydrophobia; although not named, the individual concerned was Lieutenant J. Amphlett, who died on 16 August 1817. It was also in Ireland that the 3rd Battalion Rifle Brigade was disbanded (January 1819), the officers having been placed on half-pay on 25 December 1818. In 1819 Robert married the Hon. Rebecca Massey, née Molloy, the widow of Capt. Massey, brother of Lord Massey. Following the end of his military career, Robert was employed in the constabulary but his health declined – perhaps damaged by his tribulations in the Peninsula and he died in April 1828, aged only 43.

While Robert was in Ireland, Thomas Fernyhough re-appears in the story; his regiment was disembodied in April 1816. He was married twice: his first wife, Susannah, of the Ladies' Boarding School at Rugeley, who he married in December 1804, died on the day of the birth of their sixth child, 8 July 1811 (four children survived childhood); and on 1 July 1813 Thomas married his second wife, Sarah, who ran a school for young ladies at Uttoxeter.

On 16 September 1837 Thomas was installed as a member of

the 'Lower Foundation' of the Military Knights of Windsor. Established in the 14th century, this institution maintained a small number of infirm or impoverished officers, who were originally given the duty of saying prayers daily for the sovereign and the Knights of the Order of the Garter; until 1833 they were known as the 'Poor Knights'. In 1841 Thomas was promoted to the 'Royal Foundation' of Knights, and although of only junior rank (in 1840 he was listed among the Knights as a half-pay lieutenant of the 40th), in June 1843 he was appointed as Governor (senior officer) of the Military Knights, testimony of the high regard in which he was held. Sadly, he did not long enjoy the appointment:

'1844. Jan. 8th, at the Governor's Tower, Windsor Castle, Capt. Fernyhough, Governor of the Military Knights of Windsor, aged 67. He had for some time been afflicted with a disease of the heart, and was taken ill with influenza on Friday last, and this morning, while his medical attendant, Dr. Stanford, was just in the act of administering to him some weak wine and water, he was seized with spasms of the heart, and in less than two minutes he was a corpse. Capt. Fernyhough received the appointment in June last, upon the death of the late Governor, Capt. J.J. Cumming, and was greatly beloved and respected by the whole of the Military Knights, and an extensive circle of friends in the neighbourhood of Windsor and Eton . . . He was no less distinguished as a soldier than as a man of high literary attainments. He was well known to the British Museum as a genealogist, and has left some invaluable manuscripts, relating more particularly to the topography of the county of Stafford'.[5]

He was buried with full military honours in St. George's Chapel, Windsor Castle. The literary work alluded to in his obituary was extensive: in addition to the present work, he undertook a vast amount of research on the history, genealogy and topography of his native county, and his work formed a major part of the great Staffordshire historical collection formed by William Salt, a member of a Stafford banking family (friends of the Fernyhoughs), whose archives form the core of the William Salt Library at Stafford, which was founded in 1872. Thomas's second wife, two brothers-in-law and three of his children also assisted Salt in his great enterprise. Thomas used his expertise in his subject in other ways, for example his study of the life of Samuel Johnson (a native of Lichfield), and his work on the family history of Edward Littleton, lst Baron Hatherton, who was MP for Staffordshire and subsequently Lord-Lieutenant of the county. Of all Thomas Fernyhough's work, *Military Memoirs of Four Brothers* lives on as a record of the contribution of one family to the British war effort during the Napoleonic Wars.

NOTES
1. *The Gentleman's Magazine*, February 1805, p.185.
2. ibid., December 1805, p.1172.
3. Kincaid, Sir John, *Random Shots from a Rifleman*, London 1835, p.288.
4. *The Gentleman's Magazine*, May 1812, p.498.
5. *Colburn's United Service Magazine*, 1844, Vol. I p.320.

ACKNOWLEDGEMENT
The author of this introduction wishes to express his gratitude to Randle Knight for his assistance with the genealogy of the Fernyhough family.

VALLEY OF CALIMUCHITA.

Front. ce

MILITARY MEMOIRS

OF

FOUR BROTHERS,

(NATIVES OF STAFFORDSHIRE,)

ENGAGED IN THE SERVICE OF THEIR COUNTRY,

AS WELL IN THE

NEW WORLD AND AFRICA,

AS ON THE

CONTINENT OF EUROPE.

' BY THE SURVIVOR.

LONDON:

WILLIAM SAMS, ST JAMES'S STREET,
BOOKSELLER TO THE ROYAL FAMILY.

M.DCCC.XXIX.

THESE JOURNALS

ARE RESPECTFULLY INSCRIBED TO

MAJOR-GENERAL

SIR A. F. BARNARD, K.C.B. AND K.C.H.

COLONEL OF THE FIRST BATTALION

OF

THE RIFLE BRIGADE,

BY

THE AUTHOR.

PRINTED BY J. MASTERS, ALDERSGATE STREET.

PREFACE.

THE following sheets are presented to the public by the survivor of four brothers ; three of whom have died in the military service of their country, and the fourth has been a commissioned officer upwards of thirty years. He has been encouraged in his undertaking, by the solicitations of numerous friends; and by the hope that these singular and eventful records, rendered peculiarly interesting to himself by the remembrance of the dear relatives who are the subjects of them, will be found not devoid of attraction to the general reader.

They relate to the busiest period of the late war ; and while every one is acquainted with the changes produced by that tremendous conflict, and with the events which led to them, in these Memoirs will be found an authentic narrative of the individual services and sufferings by which these mighty changes were accomplished, presenting a lively and faithful filling-up of the outline already before them in the pages of history.

Feeling his incompetency to the arduous duties of authorship, he has to solicit the indulgence of his readers for the imperfections they may discover in the execution of his work; and entreats the same candid and generous forbearance on the part of the critics of the day.

February 1829.

MILITARY MEMOIRS.

CHAPTER I.

Sketch of the Author's Life.

MY father, in his early life, was thrown upon the world by the dissipation and extravagance of his father, who inherited a small paternal property in the county of Stafford. He was addicted to gaming, which eventually brought ruin on his family. He absconded, leaving his wife dead in the house, and four children entirely destitute. They were dispersed, and when able, sought the best means in their power to provide for themselves. My father married, and settled early, and after a lapse of nearly forty years, my grandfather re-appeared.

I was talking to my father, when an aged stranger presented himself, and addressed him in these words: "Is your name F——?" My father replied in the affirmative; when he said, "I am your father!" The singularity of the appeal made a strong impression on my mind. A reconciliation took place, and after he had been sometime an inmate, he occasionally reverted to his mortgaged property, and urged my father to assist him to recover it, but he did not, or would not enter into minute particulars; and a very short time before his death, he urged me, in a solemn manner, to stimulate my father to attempt the recovery of it; but so many years had elapsed, that the transaction remains nugatory to this day.

On the augmentation of the militia in 1797, I was appointed to an ensigncy; and in 1798, received a lieutenancy in the first or western battalion of grenadiers, commanded by Lieutenant-Colonel Bradyll. This remarkably fine corps of men was formed from the grenadier companies (100 men each) of ten regiments of militia, and was encamped the same summer, on Maker Heights, in Cornwall.

In the spring of 1799, we were ordered to Winchester, when Colonel Lord G. L. G——, was so kind as to present my brother Henry, then sixteen years of age, with an ensigncy; and we both volunteered to the second battalion of the fifty-second foot, formed from the three regiments of the S—— militia, of which Lord G. L. G—— was appointed colonel, with temporary rank, and which was intended to reinforce the army in Holland, commanded by His Royal Highness the Duke of York. The retrograde movement at Alkmaar caused the English army to re-embark, and from some misunderstanding, Lord G. L. G——'s appointment was not confirmed, and in consequence the men were discharged, and the officers otherwise disposed of.

Two captains, two lieutenants, and two ensigns, were appointed to independent companies, but placed on half-pay. My brother Henry received an appointment in the S——e militia, at Windsor. As I could not immediately effect an exchange to full-pay in the line, I accepted a commission in the same regiment; and in June, 1800, was appointed a lieutenant in the light infantry.

We proceeded to Weymouth, on the King's duty, and were brigaded with several other regiments. A remarkable desertion took place from one of these: six men stole a boat out of the harbour, and put to sea; they came at length within sight of Guernsey, but being strangers to the coast, they inquired of some fishermen, if the land before them was not France. They were soon discovered by their accent to be foreigners, and the fishermen decoyed them into the port, and gave them up to a British cruiser, in the roads, as deserters, which offence they had aggravated by the commission of an act of piracy.

A general court martial sentenced two of them to be shot, and the other four to receive 1000 lashes each. The execution of their sentence soon followed. Orders were received to march at sunrise, with six rounds of ball for the field pieces, matches lighted, and the guns loaded. The brigade to have twelve rounds of ball, no reveillé to beat, nor morning gun to be fired.

The brigade arrived at Upway Downs, about seven, a. m. three miles from Weymouth. The Scots greys on the right of the line, the rifle corps

on the left, and the infantry in the centre. The guns
on the right of their respective regiments, with orders to hold themselves in readiness, should a rescue be attempted.

About eight, a. m. the dead march announced the
approach of the sufferers, at the head of their regiment, (the York hussars,) attended by two Roman
Catholic priests, in their robes and crosses. The
criminals were dressed in white, their arms pinioned,
and eighteen hussars, as executioners, commanded
by an officer, marched in the rear.

The regiment mounted in full accoutrements,
closed the procession. It is impossible, adequately,
to describe the affecting sight.

The procession slowly advanced along the front,
till it had reached the left, then countermarched,
and halted near the centre of the brigade. Major-
General Garth here produced the minutes of the
court martial, read the sentence, and the death war-
rant, in German and in English.

The loud lamentations of the sufferers were now
very distressing, the priests approached and recommended mutual forgiveness. The unfortunate men
embraced each other cordially, and the priests pronounced absolution.

The four prisoners, who were to be flogged, were
now led away, and the other two prepared to die.
They were led to their coffins, and kneeling down,
received the sacrament, and extreme unction. The
priests gradually retired, praying with them, when

the officer commanding the execution, gave three signals with his sword, and scarcely was the report of the fire-arms heard, when they ceased to exist.

The brigade was faced to the right, and marched past the bodies, in slow time, and then proceeded to Weymouth in solemn silence.

The York hussars were raised in Germany, and about 150 of them were Hungarians; their complexions very dark, and they wore large mustaches.

About this time my brother John was appointed to the Portsmouth division of marines, through the kind interest of Lord ——. In September of this year, I was gazetted on full-pay, as an ensign in the second battalion of the 60th foot, and received several recommendatory letters to the Governor of Barbadoes, the Commander-in-chief, &c.

Before my departure for the West Indies, our family met together for the last time; it was a happy period, but the retrospect is mournful; five are now numbered with the dead. It was a little singular that four brothers in the service should meet under the paternal roof at one period, destined for different parts of the globe. I should add, that my father was, at the same time, a member of the S—— yeomanry cavalry.

I now proceeded to join the depôt of my regiment in the Isle of Wight. On my arrival at Portsmouth, my brother John was in the Donegal, of eighty guns, then taking in her stores for foreign service. I engaged a boat, and was soon alongside; hailed the marine sentinel, and inquired for his officer; my brother soon made his appearance. He introduced me to his brother officers on the quarter-deck, who made me a free member of their ward-room mess. If any of these gentlemen should be living, (for it is twenty-seven years ago,) they may perhaps remember the affectionate meeting of the two brothers.

After a few days, I proceeded to East Cowes, and reported myself to Major Gomer, the commandant, who, under the old French régime, was senior lieutenant of artillery to the late king of France.

The detachments of the six battalions of the sixtieth, were composed of Russians, Poles, Germans, Italians, French, &c.; we had one Cingalese. These men were enlisted from the foreign brigade, viz. the Duc de Castre's corps, York hussars, chasseurs Britannique, le regiment de Mortemarte, and Prince Charles of Levenstein's corps, &c.

We now laid in our sea-stock, and were removed from the Isle of Wight to Fort Moncton, on the Gosport side, to hold ourselves ready for embarkation.

I take this opportunity to correct a general error regarding the sixtieth regiment. The battalions were composed entirely of foreigners, enlisted for five years, and was the only regiment in the colonies that did not receive condemned men; but all the other regiments of the line received them in quotas.

Detachments of the first, fourth, and sixth battalions now embarked for Jamaica. We accompanied our brother officers to the water's edge, shook hands, and parted, never to meet more on this side of eternity.

The Nutwel West Indiaman now arrived, and the boats of the men-of-war pulled in from Spithead to embark us. I was agreeably surprised to find my dear brother with the boats of the Donegal. The troops were soon embarked, but, owing to a strong tide and the wind blowing fresh, were carried nearly two miles to leeward of the transport, and obliged to disembark, and march back again. It was a bitter cold day.

After re-embarking, we were put on board the ship, with some difficulty, about five, p. m.

Now approached the final separation. My brother and I paced the quarter-deck of the transport, unwilling to part; the effort was great—it is past—we never met again; his revered remains are now at rest on the coast of Spain, near St. Lucar.

We now dropped down to Cowes, to take in troops from Parkhurst barracks, and on November the 9th, received on board sixty-two condemned men, to serve in various regiments in the colonies.

After a tedious passage of nine weeks, we landed at Barbadoes, and found a considerable force assembled, viz. the second and fifth battalions of the sixtieth, the sixty-fourth, and sixty-eighth regiments, the third West India, and a considerable detachment of artillery.

I had been reviewed with the sixty-eighth, the preceding year, at Swinley camp, in Windsor Forest, by his late Majesty ; the army assembled on that occasion was 22,000 men, destined for various expeditions. The two battalions of the sixty-eighth were completed to 2000 men, by volunteers from the Irish militia : they sailed for the West Indies when the camp broke up. It was about ten months since they left England when I joined the brigade to which this regiment was attached, in Barbadoes, and they had buried in Dominica and St. Lucia, 850 men, and thirty-seven commissioned officers; and eventually returned to Europe with the staff, and very few men. A brother officer, Lieutenant H——, had been private secretary to the Commander-in-chief in Martinique, he informed me, that from the commencement of the revolutionary war in 1793, to the peace of Amiens in 1801, there were buried in the windward islands only, not including the mortality of St. Domingo and Jamaica, nor the loss of human life in the various actions, about 18,000 men, and 540 commissioned officers.

As most soldiers are acquainted with the monotony of West India service, I shall pass over particulars. My health began to decline rapidly, and, after a short and severe service, I was sent by a medical board to Europe, and exchanged to half-pay in the fortieth foot.

I had arrived in England about three weeks, when Divine Providence was pleased to remove from this life, my eldest and beloved sister.—About this time, Henry was promoted to a lieutenancy in the S—— Militia, and soon after received an appointment in the Portsmouth division of royal marines, as second lieutenant, from Earl St. Vincent. His commanding officer presented him at court, at the King's levee.

He joined his corps, and was appointed to the Argo frigate, destined to convey the Mamlouk chief, Elfi Bey, out to Egypt; but receiving an accidental hurt on the side, it brought on an abscess, which proved fatal in the twenty-first year of his age, and the fifth year in his Majesty's service. He was interred at Haslar.

CHAPTER II.

Containing the Journals of Lieutenant John F——.

MY brother was appointed a second lieutenant in the Portsmouth division of marines in 1800, and embarked on board Le Juste, eighty guns, commanded by Sir Edmund Nagle.

Le Juste joined the channel fleet off Brest, on which station she remained until February 6th, 1801, when he commenced a journal, in a letter to his brother William, of a cruise to the West Indies.

On board H. M. Ship Le Juste, 80 guns,
Cawsand Bay, 3rd June, 1801.

" ACCEPT, my dear William, these lines, addressed to you from a brother, happy to inform you of his return to his native country, and hoping to be relieved from all anxiety respecting the health and happiness of his beloved friends.

Our departure from England was so sudden and unexpected, (our destination being unknown, even to the admiral, Sir Robert Calder, himself, till we arrived in a certain latitude,) that it was impossible for me to send a proper address. The French fleet consists of twenty-four sail of the line, ready for sea, in Brest harbour. Admiral Cornwallis expects they will make an attempt to sail daily, as he told the admiral commanding our squadron.

We sailed from Cawsand Bay on the 6th of February, 1801; on the 9th, saw nine sail to windward of us, and on the 10th, came up with them, and the in-shore squadron, close in with the French coast.

We received orders to join the nine sail, under the command of Sir Robert Calder, making seven sail of the line, two frigates, and one brig. We parted company with the in-shore squadron that evening, to go in quest of the French fleet, commanded by Admiral Ganthaume.

Crossing the Bay of Biscay, we discovered the Spanish coast, Cape Finisterre, encountering a heavy gale, which lasted three days. The squadron parted company, except the admiral and our ship: four sail rejoined us on the 17th; the Montague, seventy-four guns, and the Magicienne frigate, had their masts carried away during the gale; they were obliged to bear up before the wind.

The brig we never heard of afterwards, and fear she foundered in the storm, and all hands perished. Our ship for two days was continually flooded; the sea stove in the larboard quarter gallery, and the ward-room had three windows stove in; the sea broke over the quarter-deck, and carried away one of the boats on the larboard quarter.

We bore up for Lisbon after the storm, with seven sail out of the ten, and arrived there on the 19th; we found the Montague in the Tagus, dismasted, but the frigate we did not see again till we arrived at Jamaica. We made Cape St. Vincent on the 22nd, and altered our sailing W. by S., concluding our course was bent for the West Indies.

We saw from the mast-head on the 25th, seventy-two sail, outward bound, came up with them on the 26th, and made the island of Madeira. Our squadron lay-to before Funchal, and took in bullocks and wine for the ship's company. The next day, the governor and consul paid the admiral a visit, and informed him that five sail of the line, and five frigates were seen off the island on the 24th.

On the 27th, we bore away from Madeira, steering for Teneriffe, supposing the enemy to be there. We made the Peak, about eighteen leagues, on the 1st of March, though rather hazy; but in clear weather, it may be seen at the distance of more than fifty leagues. We arrived before the island in the evening, when the admiral made signal to clear for action, and to anchor, expecting to find the French fleet in the Bay of Santa Cruz, which is the principal town in the island, and extremely well fortified.

Early in the morning of the 2nd, we were well in with the land, all ready for action, and at our quarters. Signal was made to form line of battle in open order, and a frigate was sent to reconnoitre the harbour, to see if the enemy was there; she made a signal to the admiral, 'No enemy in sight.'

Judge of our disappointment, all our castles were built in the air. I was stationed with a party of marines, on the quarter-deck, at the carronades, and we were to take up small arms, when occasion required, to annoy the enemy with volleys of musketry; but all our expectations vanished at the sight of the signal.

I had packed up all my trunks, and made a memorandum in my pocket book, where to send them, had I fallen in this expected conflict.

We bore up from Teneriffe, cruising among the Canary Isles for three or four days, and then bent our course to the West Indies. We crossed the tropic of Cancer on the 9th of March, and entered the torrid zone, when I was much amused with the novel sight of the flying fish, grampusses, and dolphins.

We arrived at Barbadoes on the 24th, lay-to for some hours, then proceeded to Martinique, and anchored in Cáse de Nevere's Bay. We took in wood and water, and sailed on the 29th, in search of Admiral Duckworth's squadron; passed most of the Antilles, and found the squadron before St. Thomas's, which it had just captured from the Danes; we parted company, and made Porto Rico, on the 2nd of April. We came to an anchor in Port Royal, Jamaica, on the 12th.—After remaining a short time under the command of Lord Hugh Seymour, we received on board French and Spanish prisoners, and sailed from Jamaica on the 21st; came through the windward passage, instead of stretching along the coast of America. We joined the grand fleet, off Ushant,

on the 2nd of June and received orders from Admiral
Cornwallis to repair to Cawsand Bay, where we arrived this morning, at five o'clock, 3rd of June; having
been just six weeks on our passage from Jamaica."

My gallant brother continued on the Irish station
for sometime, when the mutiny broke out at Bantry
Bay, and the fleet proceeded to England with the
mutineers. His health became much impaired from
active service, when he obtained leave of absence,
and came to his native county.

He rejoined his corps at Portsmouth, June the 9th,
1802.—On the 19th, he was appointed to the Donegal, eighty guns, commanded by Sir Richard
Strachan.

CHAPTER III.

Journal continued.—His services in the Mediterranean.

On January the 25th, 1803, the Donegal weighed
anchor from Spithead, and we proceeded to the
Mediterranean—spoke the Cynthia, off Cape St.
Vincent; this part of the Spanish coast is apparently barren and uncultivated, with a bold shore; from
this cape, the Spaniards beheld the destruction of
their fleet, 14th February, 1797.

We came to an anchor in Gibraltar Bay, on
February 4th; Sir R. Strachan, and Lieut.-Col. Far-
mer, went on shore to pay their respects to the
Governor, His Royal Highness the Duke of Kent.

We got under weigh for Malta, sailed along the
eastern shore of Spain : the lofty mountains of Grenada (which province is bounded by the Mediterranean on the eastward) present themselves in
majestic grandeur, their towering summits clothed
in snow.

Passed the islands of St. Peter, Antioch, Vache,
and Mount Toro;—made the island of Sardinia,
whose lofty mountains capped with snow, have a
grand effect.

I observed on the night of the 11th of February, on
the first watch, an unusual phenomenon in the moon;

it first assumed the semblance of a volcano, emitting lava, and afterwards a pale transparent colour, intersected with dark streaks of clouds:—running down the S. W. coast of Sicily.

At one, p. m. came abreast the island of Malta; went on shore to visit Valette, its suburbs, and the church of St. John. The streets are regular, and the houses of a uniform design, built of white stone. The Grand Master's palace is a stately structure, occupying a great space of ground, and having a large square in front. The hotels of the knights are worthy of notice, being elegantly ornamented with sculpture and statuary; most of them have verandas to make them cool and airy.

The stradas are well paved with flat stones, but not spacious. They are partly inhabited by Greeks, who are a fine race of men, having but little intercourse with the Maltese, although the latter are courteous and affable towards strangers. Their complexions are of an olive colour; in form, they are generally stout and athletic; in disposition, prone to impose.

Their dress consists of trowsers, sandals, cotton or stuff jackets, cap or handkerchief on the head; and in cold weather a surtout or cloak thrown over the shoulders, lined with a shaggy stuff resembling hair.

The women of the better class are dressed mostly in black silk. The gentlemen and tradesmen dress like the English.

The fortifications of Valette and its environs, are superior to any in the known world for strength and construction. On entering the harbour, I was much struck with the stupendous buildings, rising in noble majesty to the view, in successive tiers, one above another.

It being the carnival at Malta, the inhabitants appear in the streets masked. In the course of my walk, I observed that the Maltese treated all the British officers with deference and respect, though they are not so delicate in their behaviour towards officers of other nations.

The English admiral and general, have each splendid apartments allotted them in the late Grand Master's palace. The governor resides in a palace of one of the knights.

Issola was founded before Valette, and though not so extensive, the buildings have the appearance of equal grandeur. The opera-house at Valette, is of considerable magnitude, in a central situation : during the carnival, it was appropriated to masked balls. On the 23rd, the Diana frigate arrived from Constantinople, with the Earl of Elgin.

I visited the towns of Florian and Burmala, adjacent to Valette. In strolling through them, I was induced to look into the churches, and found them ornamented in a costly manner. At particular times they are decorated with crimson damask and velvet.

It being Lent, I had an opportunity of seeing

c

some paintings, representing the passion of our Saviour on the mount, which, according to my judgment, were well executed. I observed several boxes, resembling sentry boxes, which are appropriated to the priests, and in which they hear confession.

I visited the state rooms of the palace of the Grand Master, at Valette. They are lofty and spacious, with a profusion of gilt carved work, statuary, and paintings, consisting of landscape, historical, and scriptural subjects. Some of the apartments are hung with rich damask and tapestry; but to make their magnificence complete, they require a little more furniture, the want of which is conspicuous in every house in the island. The zodiac room, (so called from the twelve signs delineated on the floor,) is superior to them all; there is a collection of paintings in it, representing the siege of the island by the Turks, when they were repulsed with dreadful slaughter. This apartment also contains the throne of the Grand Master.

We made an excursion into the interior as far as Civita Vecchia, formerly the principal residence of the Grand Master and knights; it is about eight miles from Valette. The island having little or no wood, affords but an indifferent prospect to the eye of an Englishman, accustomed to the luxuriance of his own country.

The towns of Valette, Issola, &c., are supplied with water by an aqueduct, on the road to Civita

Vecchia; it is built of white stone. We observed
a number of good-looking houses, uninhabited,
which might be rented for two shillings per week,
for which £50. per annum would probably be demanded in England.   The Grand Master has a
palace called St. Antoine.   We arrived at Civita
Vecchia about eleven, a. m.; our first visit was to
St. Paul's church, a stately building, but not so
magnificent as St. John's, at Valette.   The high
altar is little inferior, but the pavement will not bear
the slightest comparison.

From the church, we went to the college of the
same name, founded on the cave where St. Paul
is reported to have taken refuge. We followed our
guide, and descended a flight of steps by torch-light,
and entered the cave, hewn out of the solid rock,
in which is the statue of St. Paul.   This cave is
about thirty yards in circumference. I cut my name
on the roof.

We then explored the catacombs, which are worth
the observation of the curious.   Far in the recess is
a chapel, rudely cut in the rock; there are also
places cut which resemble coffins.   These ancient
caverns extend seven miles.

We afterwards visited the Bank of Registry, and
then the spot where the Maltese massacred the
French; they are said to have devoured the flesh of
their victims, to evince their implacable hatred. We
viewed the fortifications of Victoriosi, which are

considered impregnable, and was defended by the garrison against the Turks, when they had possessed themselves of the island; the angle facing the sea, has three tiers of batteries, rising one above another; the first is called the water-line battery, being almost level with the sea, and did much execution during the siege.

We began to prepare for our departure, and on May 18, 1803, unmoored at three, a. m. and put to sea with a fine breeze. Our squadron consisted of nine sail of the line, viz. Kent, 74, (flag-ship); Renown, 74; Donegal, 80; Triumph, 74; Superb, 74; Monmouth, 74; Agincourt, 74; Gibraltar, 80; Belle-isle, 74; and Cyclops, trooper. We passed the port of Syracuse on the 20th; saw Mount Ætna, but observed very little eruption. We came close in with the land under it on the 22nd, and had a distinct and perfect view of it. The stupendous grandeur of the scene cannot fail to impress the mind with astonishment; its lofty summit, towering high above the clouds, and its dark crater, emitting immense volumes of smoke, form a singular contrast with the delicate whiteness of the region of snow which surrounds it.

Below its summit are rugged rocks, but around its base the country is remarkably picturesque and beautiful; to describe it adequately is beyond the power of my pen. The dark purple shade on the mountain, increased, if possible, the resplendent beauties of the heavens : it was a scene surpassing description, and called forth my adoration of the great Creator of such stupendous and lovely objects.

We entered the Straits of Messina on the 23rd. The town is built on the declivity of a hill : the houses are erected one above another, and have a fine appearance. It is pretty well fortified. The country around is mountainous and luxuriant in the extreme; the opposite coast of Calabria presents a similar aspect.

I observed on this coast, three towns of considerable size ; their external appearance resembled Messina, and there seems to be very little difference in their construction, being generally flat-roofed, and of white stone. The width of the Straits is about three or four miles, and in the middle runs a very strong current, which affected our ship (though a large one) very much, and even caused a vertical motion for a short time. Vessels of a smaller burden have been whirled round with great and dangerous rapidity.

We cleared the Straits, and approached the Lipari Isles and Mount Stromboli, another volcano. The Italian shore, and that of Sicily, are bold and mountainous, and covered with verdure from the base to the mountain tops.

About seven, p. m. we neared Stromboli, about fifty miles from the Straits, which gave us an opportunity of seeing it vomiting flames. On the north side is the crater, from which flows the lava; at first

it emitted smoke only, but about eight, p. m. fire became visible, increasing in magnitude every minute.
Some explosions took place, which had a very grand
effect, dispersing particles of a black substance.
The diameter of this flaming stream, which exhibited
a magnificent and awful spectacle, could not be less
than fourteen feet.   When night had spread her sa-
ble mantle over the heavens, and obscured the land
from our eyes, this burning lake assumed a different
form, and became, as it were, a vast pillar of fire.
The mountain is nearly of a conical form.

On the 30th we had a distant view of Vesuvius.
A royal salute was fired on the 4th of June, being
the birth-day of our most gracious Sovereign; at
three, p. m. arrived the Niger, with intelligence of
war having been declared by England against
France and Holland, on the 21st of May.   In consequence of which, we bent our course towards
Elba, with the fleet, to watch the motions of the
enemy.

Our spirits were buoyant, and we prepared in good
earnest to come into conflict with the enemy; my
brother officers were anxious to display their courage
in the cause of their king and country, and we had
the most implicit confidence in the talents of our
excellent commander, Sir Richard Strachan.   The
Donegal, which he commanded, was as fine a floating battery of 80 guns, on two decks, as any in His
Majesty's service.

There were times, when I could not help thinking

of my dear and excellent parents, who had now four sons in the service, anxious to do all in their power to raise the respectability of their family. I thought, the fortune of war might possibly spare us, or that blanks might be made in our affectionate family circle: but to God I committed the future, submitting all to his divine and unerring will. It is just one month since I completed my twenty-fourth year.

On the 6th of June, came abreast of Rome,—land in sight,—fired volleys of musketry to exercise our small arms,—chased two vessels,—passed the islands of Elba, Cabrara, Brade, and Corsica. This latter has a barren and mountainous aspect, and the summits of the mountains were then covered with snow.

We received intelligence on the 11th, of the French fleet, ten sail of the line, and four frigates; began to clear away for action. We came in sight of Toulon, with a view of the Alps, which divide France from Italy, though we could not have been less than eighty miles from them. Standing off and on Toulon, exercising our great guns.

On the 27th we were close in, and the Renown standing towards the land, made signal of seeing six men-of-war in the outer roads, ready for sea. We stood in closer with the fleet. The Amphion frigate joined us on the 8th of July, with Lord Nelson on board, from Malta, to take the command of the fleet.

The squadron ordered to close round the admiral,

and signal for all captains.   The French fleet reconnoitred by the Maidstone, and found to be seven
sail of the line, five frigates, and five corvettes.   We
received intelligence of the war with Spain, on the
25th ; stood over to the Bay of Rosas, on the Spanish
coast, to cover the Renown, while watering.

We received on board, on the 10th, Mr. A'Court,
our charge d'affaires at Naples, and were ordered to
proceed with him to Barcelona.   His Majesty's ship
Canopus hove in sight on the 15th, with Admiral
Campbell on board, to join Lord Nelson.   The Ter-
magant came down to speak us ; at seven came on a
storm, with thunder and lightning, for the space of
two hours, which was very awful ; found ourselves
close under the island of Yvica.

We boarded, on the 20th of August, a fine Danish
vessel from Leghorn, bound to Lisbon.   I requested
Sir Richard Strachan to allow me to go on board
her, with which he complied.   On boarding the
Dane, we were shown into the cabin, and there saw
a gentleman in bed, and another standing by him.
I accosted the latter in French, and learned that the
gentleman in bed was a cardinal, going on an em-
bassy from the Pope to Lisbon, and that the person
to whom I was speaking was his secretary.

He appeared a gentlemanlike man, and his manners engaging ; we requested him to open his baggage, in order that it might be inspected, as it was
the custom of the British service in order to detect
any illicit trade.   There were also two Dominican

friars, going to Africa to promulgate the Gospel. Allowed the Dane to proceed.

We descried a man-of-war on the 21st, standing off the Spanish coast, altered our course to fall in with her; at seven, p. m., drum beat to quarters. We were taking our wine after dinner, in the ward-room; upon this signal, the bulk heads were knocked down, fore and aft guns loaded, and matches lighted, the ship carrying a heavy press of sail.

We neared the chase very fast, fired a gun to bring her to; at half-past eleven came up with her, hailed, and sent a boat on board. She proved to be a Spanish frigate, from Cadiz to Carthagena; she had also cleared for action. After beating the retreat, retired at half-past twelve.

Spoke an American frigate on a cruise. Saw the rock of Gibraltar on the 28th, and stood into the bay, anchoring off the old mole : employed taking in stores. Came on board, September 3rd, Elfi Bey, the Mamlouk chief, to visit our captain. He was going to England in quality of ambassador; he was richly dressed, in crimson and yellow, with scimitar and dagger, yellow and white turban, and yellow morocco boots. He had a noble aspect, a commanding figure, and his deportment very majestic; an interpreter attended him.

We steered, on the 9th, towards Cadiz, descried the light-house, and the Maidstone at anchor; stood close in on the 10th, to order the Maidstone to weigh anchor, and come within hail, and ordered her to cruise off the harbour, then parted company. We heard, from a Swedish vessel, that Buonaparte had arrested Moreau.

A man-of-war hove in sight at half-past six; beat to quarters, and cleared for action; made the private signal, and not being answered, prepared to give her a broadside, she came down on our weather bow, and passed to windward. We now gave her a broadside, which brought her to on her starboard quarter. She then hailed us in Spanish, and sent an officer with a boat on board, and, to our great satisfaction, heard that she had no men killed or wounded; but we had damaged her mizen mast. We afterwards fell in with a large ship, which proved to be a cartel from Cape François, with Admiral Latouche and suite on board, bound to Marseilles. His health having been much impaired, he had leave from the First Consul; allowed her to proceed. Stood close in with the African shore, which presented but a dreary prospect.

CHAPTER IV.

*Journal continued.—Of service in the Mediterranean, from
January* 20, *to December* 31, 1804.

IN commencing the new year, we bore up for Gibraltar, and came to an anchor in the bay at four,
p. m. On the 23rd, the Diana frigate came in, firing
guns, as a signal, to give intelligence of a French
line-of-battle ship, and two corvettes, having sailed
from Cadiz. We unmoored and got under weigh,
in company with the Medusa, all clear for battle,
steering for Cadiz, lying all night at our quarters,
and arrived at three, a. m.

On the 24th, stood in close to reconnoitre, and
found the enemy as before. We fell in with and
spoke the Argo, from England, with Elfi Bey and
his suite on board, bound for Egypt.

We now steered along the eastern coast of Corsica,
and saw four sail close in to the land. On a nearer
view, found them to be large frigates, made all possible sail, and gave chase; the Amazon being in
company, did so likewise; cleared for action, and
made signal for battle.

After a long and tedious pursuit came up with them, and to our great mortification, they proved to be the Narcissus and Juno frigates. They took us for a French line-of-battle ship and a frigate.

It blew very hard on the 7th of February, accompanied with rain. We descried two sail coming down before the wind, tacked, and stood for them; at three, p. m. discovered five more, which, on close inspection, proved to be the fleet under Lord Nelson; spoke the Admiral.

The cold was intense this day, the 8th; came on a gale; steered for the Magdalen isles, for security; at twelve, came to an anchor with the fleet. This bay being more capacious than Agincourt Bay, is called 'Grand Bay;' there is room enough for a large fleet to ride in safety.

The Sardinians came alongside with vegetables, fruits, bread, &c., but every thing was very dear, occasioned solely by the prodigality of the English. The islanders are stout and athletic, well formed, and hardy in constitution. We procured a boat from the captain, and made an excursion to the principal town of the islands, near Agincourt Sound, or outer bay.

Myrtles, and a variety of aromatic shrubs and flowers, grow here spontaneously. The women are very handsome, of agreeable manners, and appear to be courteous. The men are mountaineers, and have the semblance of hardihood. No man is without his gun, by means of which he supports himself. One of the islands contiguous to Sardinia, and forming part of the bay where we anchored, was colonized by a party of Corsicans and Sardinians, about thirty years ago, with this franchise from the King of Sardinia,—that they should enjoy the produce of their lands, &c., free from taxation or any impost whatever, for one century. They have built a town called St. Pierre, the houses of which are of white stone, and neatly constructed.

They were attacked a short time ago, by some Algerine corsairs, who came to destroy their property; but they collected themselves in a body, and bravely repelled the barbarians, with considerable slaughter. I went into one of their chapels, and was astonished to see so many beautiful women. The bread we got was superior to any I ever met with; instead of making it with water, they use goat's milk, which gives it an excellent flavour.

The signal was made at six, a. m. on the 19th, to weigh anchor for sea. We got under weigh at eight, and the fleet put to sea, clearing the islands at ten. We closed in with the island of Minorca the next day, and came into smooth water, abreast of Port Mahon, the principal port in the island, on the south east end. This is supposed to be the most commodious harbour in the Mediterranean, except Malta; the entrance is so well fortified by nature, as well as by art, as to be considered almost impregnable.

We anchored again on the 25th of March, in

Agincourt Sound, and found two galleys before the
town, belonging to the King of Sardinia, one of
which was the Admiral, having on board 350 men;
the oars are plied by slaves. I inquired what were
their crimes, and was informed they were chiefly
condemned for murder; they were heavily ironed.
These galleys resemble those described by Homer
and Virgil: one broadside from a British man-of-war
would blow them out of the water. The commander
came on board, to visit our noble admiral, Lord
Nelson.

We got under weigh on the 5th of April, and
put to sea at five, p. m.; came close under the high
land of Corsica; signal, three sail a-head. The
Victory, Canopus, Donegal, and Belleisle, and two
frigates, went in chase. At seven, a. m. on the 9th,
saw four sail and a large convoy, three of the four
were frigates, and one line-of-battle ship: discovered
them to be French. We immediately gave chase
with the Active, to cover the retreat of the Amazon,
with a prize which she had taken from the convoy,
in sight of the enemy, standing close in to the land.
The French seemed disposed to attack the Amazon;
she brought-to, to receive their fire, though of inferior
force. After standing on a little, they tacked, and
stood in again. We bore up, and followed them
close into the harbour of Toulon. The French fleet
prepared to weigh, and at four, p. m. one line-of-
battle ship came out, as we thought, to attack us.
We beat to quarters, and soon cleared for action.

The enemy formed line at five, with gun-boats in their rear, standing under easy sail. At six, three more line-of-battle ships got under weigh, standing out of the harbour. We made signal to our fleet for assistance; the enemy's force being four sail of the line and three frigates, ours only one sail of the line and two frigates. The Superb and Excellent bore down to join us. At eight, p.m. the enemy tacked, and stood in again; we pursued, under the fire of the batteries on the shore. At nine we stood out again, observing the enemy's motions till the morning. Signal to return to the fleet.

Steering for the Spanish coast, at four came off Barcelona; lay-to in the Bay of Rosas, and on the 13th bore up again for Toulon. Lay-to, on the 18th, in the Gulf of Genoa, standing close in to the land, under the mountains of Savoy.

Again receiving orders to reconnoitre the harbour of Toulon, parted company from the fleet, and stood close in to the outer roads; discovered five sail of the line; at seven stood close in; the batteries opened their fire upon us; standing off and on. At eleven, brought-to a small vessel, bound to Corsica, from Marseilles, laden with merchandize; took out the prisoners, with their own property, and set fire to the vessel and cargo.

We now prepared for action, and stood in for the shore; at six, received several shots from the batteries; chased a French frigate, and opened a heavy fire upon her, which was quickly returned by the bat-

teries. We received a shot through the royal sail,
and another fell close under our larboard quarter,
which occasioned the water to rise and fall like a
shower of rain on the deck.

We soon brought our guns to bear, and handsomely returned the compliment, with the British
thunder. This was kept up with equal spirit for
some time, till three line-of-battle ships got under
weigh to chase us off the coast, which followed us
for some distance, and then tacked. At four, p. m. we
stood in again, and poured a volley of shot amongst
some boats under the land, which we thought were
armed.

The batteries now saluted us with shot and
shells; we returned their civilities with our broadsides, then wished them good night, and stood off
till morning. On the 28th, we returned to reconnoitre the enemy, and counted seven sail of the line
and six frigates.

We had an excellent prospect of the harbour,
and country around : to the right, is a stately castle,
apparently very ancient. The fortifications seemed
to be strong. Rejoined the fleet. We sailed for
Corsica; 11th of May, at six, p. m. entered the Straits
of Bonafacio, and anchored in Agincourt Sound.

How can I express the grief I felt, on hearing
from England of the death of my beloved sister,
and of my brother Henry, at Portsmouth? and how
singular, that I should have fallen in twice with the
Argo frigate, at Gibraltar, to which he was ap-

pointed a lieutenant of marines? God is merciful! Man was not born to lead a life of supineness and inactivity, but, as a probationer on earth, to endure the chequered scenes of prosperity and adversity. My prayer to God is, that he would enable me to bear with fortitude all the changes of this mortal life. I learnt also, that my eldest brother is arrived from the West Indies; and I sincerely congratulate him on his escape from that fatal climate.

We sailed along the shores of Sardinia. Our chaplain, myself, and a brother officer, landed, and made a short excursion into the country. We met a number of mountaineers, clad in a singular manner, presenting, altogether, a most grotesque appearance. Every man was armed with a musket and stiletto, and well mounted. The roads to the mountains appeared to me almost impassable, not only from their ruggedness, but from the great quantity of bushes; but these men led the way, and went through them with the utmost facility; their horses, from custom, cautiously climb and descend the most frightful precipices, with the greatest safety.

At the cottages, we procured milk, curds, honey, and cakes baked on ashes, afterwards washed in milk. Grapes grow spontaneously in the valleys, but were not yet ripe. Their principal riches consist in their flocks and herds.

We unmoored and put to sea, May 18th; steered for Terra Nuova, on the eastern coast of Sardinia; and at three, p. m. anchored in a very capacious bay,

D

surrounded by immense rocks and mountains. We
weighed anchor at eight next morning, and bent our
course for Toulon. Parted company with the Canopus, to reconnoitre the harbour.

We neared the land on the 23rd; descried three
frigates, and one line-of-battle ship, at the entrance.
The Canopus commenced firing on the frigate nearest to us,—tacked, and stood off the land under
easy sail; when two more line-of-battle ships were
observed coming out, and standing after us.

The frigate most a-head now and then returned
the fire of the Canopus, but without damage. At
twelve, the headmost line-of-battle ship luffed up,
to give us a broadside, which was as ineffectual
as the frigate's. We now luffed up in the wind,
and commenced a smart fire on the frigate, which
had considerable effect. We afterwards kept up
a running fire with the enemy, endeavouring to
draw him out from the land, as by this means we
hoped to cut some of them off; but they tacked,
and stood in again. We then bore away to join
our admiral, Lord Nelson. The Victory, Excellent,
and Leviathan, parted company on the 27th, to
reconnoitre the French fleet; they rejoined us on the
30th. We again appeared before Toulon, on June
1st, and cleared for action. June 4th. This being
the King's birth-day, at one, p. m. fired a royal salute
in the enemy's teeth; and had he come out during
our effusions of loyalty, he would have paid dear
for his temerity. We now observed the French

fleet making preparations to come out;—lay-to. At ten, three sail appeared at the mouth of the harbour; and at twelve, five ships hauled out.

We received information, that two of the enemy's ships were lying in Hieres Bay; sent the Phœbe and Amazon to reconnoitre. At three, p.m. the enemy's fleet was observed getting under weigh. At five, p.m. saw twelve ships of the line, and some frigates, standing out. Our feelings were highly excited, and our joy inexpressible, when at half-past five, our admiral gave signal to prepare for battle, to anchor, man launches, and to arm the boats.

Now for the glorious conflict, for the honour of old England and her wooden walls! The enemy still advancing, apparently to attack us; the English fleet lying-to, to receive him, off Hieres, tacking and wearing occasionally. After thus gasconading, at eight, the French fleet tacked, and stood in again, and would not fight us.

Next morning, a part of the enemy's fleet appeared again, at the mouth of the harbour; but showing no disposition to come out, we bore away to join the remaining part of the fleet under admiral Sir Richard Bickerton. Fell in with three transports, laden with provisions, and captured them. We heard a distant cannonading; supposing it to be the squadron of frigates in-shore, at three, p.m. signal for all launches, manned and armed, to repair on board. 23rd. Joined the Narcissus and Childers brig, with a prize in tow, taken in Hieres Bay:

brought an account of the frigates having been attacked by a number of French gun-boats, which
were beaten off.   Observed a number of lights on
shore and along the coast.

We were detached on the 16th of July, and ordered
to proceed to the rendezvous, and remain twenty-
four hours, to observe if any vessel had arrived from
England ; received intelligence of a convoy ; bore
up on the 30th, for the Gulf of Palma, in Sardinia,
and at nine, p. m. came to an anchor.

I made an excursion on shore ; found the country
quite in an uncultivated state, excepting a few vine-
yards, which afforded plenty of red and white
grapes, hanging in clusters eighteen inches in length.
Houses are not to be seen scattered on the coast, as
in England, for fear of the Barbary corsairs, but the
people generally live in small towns, and never go
from home unarmed. The islanders, or rather mountaineers, are a fine robust race of men, and appear to
be inoffensive in their manners. The Bay, or Gulf of
Palma, is a remarkably fine anchorage, capacious and
well protected.

Signal to prepare for sea on the 6th of August.   At
eight, made sail for Cagliari, but stood off for the
night.   In the morning at eight, came to an anchor,
five leagues from the town, which we could but
slightly discern; it appeared to be built on an eminence.   Employed in watering the fleet on the adjacent shore ; went to reconnoitre the country. Fruits
seem to be the principal produce, and are abundant;

as grapes, melons, pumpions, pears, mulberries, figs, almonds, &c. The south end of the island is by far the most fertile.

We weighed anchor on the 11th, and stood out to sea; received intelligence of a victory over the French fleet off Brest; we made a reconnoissance at Toulon; heard of the defeat of the French admiral, Latouche Tourelle. We parted company from the fleet on the 13th of October; made the island of Majorca on the 16th, and arrived at Gibraltar on the 20th; lay-to in the bay, to get information.

We were soon apprised of the mortality of the garrison and inhabitants, from the effects of a contagious fever, which raged with great fury. They had lost upwards of 2,000 people. Having made our observations, we sailed for Cadiz; we spoke the Medusa frigate on the 21st, and learnt from her that three valuable Spanish frigates, laden with specie, had been captured by our ships, but that one was unfortunately blown up. Orders arrived on the 23rd, to suffer no Spanish ship of war to proceed outward bound, but to enjoin them to return into port, and in case of refusal, to capture them, and send them to England.

We soon had an opportunity of making a prize; at ten, discovered a Spanish frigate from Cadiz, called the Matilda, laden with quicksilver, for South America. We communicated our orders to her, giving a specified time for consideration, at the same time ordering her to strike; not complying, a few shot were fired over her, which had the desired effect of intimidation; she struck, and we took possession of her, and despatched her to England, in charge of the Medusa, she being in company. We did not molest their trade, but continued to cruise off and on the coast, in hopes of falling in with a treasure-ship, which was daily expected.

On the 13th of November, after cruising on the Spanish coast for some time, at three, p. m. fell in and spoke with the William transport, from Gibraltar to England, with passengers. We procured a statement of the mortality on the rock: died, since September, 3,000 inhabitants, and upwards of 700 soldiers, and forty officers. Observed a man-of-war on the 14th, which at ten joined us, and proved to be the Defence, seventy-four guns, from England; we parted company at six; we afterwards fell in with the Leviathan, Agamemnon, Ruby, and Polyphemus, from England, admiral Sir John Orde.

We received orders on the 17th to join Lord Nelson; made sail, and at the decline of the day, just on entering the Gut of Gibraltar, we descried a man-of-war, coming down before the wind; we signalized to her, and demanded her number, and upon her not answering the private signal, we instantly beat to quarters, to clear for action, conceiving her to be a French man-of-war, called L'Aigle, which had been in Cadiz many months, waiting an opportunity to escape. What made her more suspicious, she altered her course to avoid us; we endeavoured to cut her off, but her good sailing frustrated our intentions ; notwithstanding we persisted in the chase, along the western shore of Africa. Lay at our quarters all night; 18th, at daylight, we were enabled to discover and ascertain her force and magnitude.

She proved to be a Spanish frigate, of forty guns ; at this time she was under an immense press of sail, right before the wind ; on the morning of the 19th to our great satisfaction we perceived that her foretop gallant mast, had sustained some injury, which deprived her of the use of those sails, so that we gained upon her very fast; and at nine, a. m. came up with her, fired a shot to make her bring-to ; desired the captain to come on board, or send a boat, representing the purport of our orders to him, with a limited time for consideration. At this period we were ready for action, and had been at our quarters from the commencement of the chase. After the officer's return, receiving no reply, orders were given to fire upon the frigate; which she most gallantly retorted. We then opened our broadside and musketry, and after an action of ten or twelve minutes, she hauled down the Spanish colours, and struck to our superior force. We took possession of her, and to our sorrow, found that her brave captain was killed by a musket shot, which had penetrated his heart ; three men were killed, besides considerable damage done to the ship. We returned to Gibraltar with our prize. She had 370 men

on board, 270 of which were removed on board the
Donegal, for fear of bad consequences.

She was called the Amphitrite. The officers were
permitted to remain on board, which is not usually
allowed, but the Spanish officers were gentlemanly
men, and their courage deserved this consideration.
Their uniforms were splendid, though not elegant,
having too much lace about them.

The action took place off Mogador, on the coast
of Africa. The Amphitrite was bound to Teneriffe,
and from thence to South America, with despatches.
At three, p. m. committed the body of the brave but
unfortunate Spanish captain to the deep, with the
honours of war. The chase lasted forty hours, running a distance of 301 miles.

On the 25th, spoke the Polyphemus, and received
orders to take, burn, and destroy all Spanish vessels.
We took a Spanish vessel on the 26th, laden with
hides and tallow. In capturing this vessel, two
men-of-war hove in sight, who will share with us,
according to the established custom of the Navy.
We spoke the Polyphemus on the 2nd of November,
she informed us that she had taken a valuable prize,
laden with dollars, &c.

On the 5th of December, prepared to beat through
the Gut of Gibraltar; after making frequent attempts,
we accomplished it about twelve at night. Came to
an anchor with our prizes, the Spanish frigate and
ship; proceeded to Algesiras, to adjust matters respect-

ing the prisoners; at three, p. m. boats arrived to take them away; the officers were on parole.

To our great satisfaction, we found the inhabitants of the rock greatly improved in health. We were informed that the number which perished, of military and civilians, amounted to 4,500 souls. We made demand for provisions, &c. Employed on the 9th in mooring our frigate, and other prize.

Joined on the 13th, the Halcyon and Leviathan, when we heard that an embargo had been laid on all English ships at Lisbon.

Nothing particular transpired, excepting the occurrences of very active service,—keeping the sea, and overhauling ships of different nations; we had but little respite, as every day seemed eventful. The year closed without our meeting the fleet of the enemy.

CHAPTER V.

*Journal continued, from January, to October 26th, 1805, four
days after the battle of Trafalgar, when Lieutenant John
F——, lost his life off St. Lucar.*

On January 19th, 1805, the Active hove in sight,
with intelligence of the enemy's fleet having sailed
from Toulon, which chased her off that port. Signal
made for the fleet to weigh anchor, and put to sea.
At seven, went through the Narrows, an enterprise never before attempted in the British navy.
20th. Signal to prepare for battle, running or beating down the eastern coast of Sardinia. The Amphion arrived on the 21st, with intelligence of the
enemy being in the Gulf of Cagliari; bent our
course thither; looked into the gulf, but saw no
enemy: lay-to for intelligence. At four, p. m. made
sail again. On the 26th, joined the Phœbe, with
an account of three of the enemy's fleet having got
into Adjano, with the loss of their topmasts. At
four, made sail for Sicily; saw Monetino and C.
Vito : standing along shore.

Joined by the Phœbe, Anson, and Tigre, the latter
from Palermo; sent there for intelligence of the
enemy—received none. At eight, a. m. 28th, stood

into the Gulf of Palermo; saw Stromboli to the
N. E. at a great distance, by the crater emitting
fire.   The Seahorse frigate arrived on the 29th from
Naples.   Still no tidings of the enemy.   Made signals for pilots, to work through the Straits of Messina.   Cleared Cape Spartienti.

The Faro, or light house, is at the N. E. end, or
mouth of the Straits, situated on a low flat point, on
the Sicilian shore; the opposite coast of Calabria,
is bold and lofty, interspersed with towns and
villages.   The towns most deserving of notice are
Scylla and Reggio; the former so much celebrated
in ancient history.

The Sicilian shore far surpasses that of Calabria
in verdure and luxuriance; and it abounds with
elegant mansions, particularly in the vicinity of
Messina.   The city is of great extent; there are
two commanding forts at the back of it, and it appears to be well fortified towards the sea.

The dreadful ravages of the earthquake are still
perceptible in the ruins of many superb edifices on
each side of the city.   We continued our pursuit of
the enemy.

Land discovered on February 1st, to the N.E.,
being the S. W. end of the Morea.   We passed
Candia on the 3rd, renowned for its defence against
the Turks, from 1645 to 1649.   The Ottomans lost
180,000 men, and the Venetians 80,000, before it
capitulated.   We passed close to that part of Egypt
formerly called Lybia, on the 5th; and now the

desert of Barca, a level country to the west of
Alexandria.   The Tigre and Anson sent a-head to
look out; signal, having gained soundings.   Steered towards the city of Alexandria on the 7th.   The
Tigre ordered close in for intelligence.

We could see distinctly the most conspicuous
buildings, Pompey's pillar, and some public works.
Alexandria is built on a neck of land, forty miles
west of the Nile.   Three Turkish men-of-war were
lying in the harbour.   At six, made sail to the
westward, running nine knots : standing off and on.
Candia in sight on the 13th.   Little can be said of
its fertility; shore bold and lofty, and the country
mountainous.   The Morea in sight; passed the
S. W. end of Sicily, Malta, and Goza; and learned
that the French fleet had put back to Toulon.
A pretty run they have given us.

Close in with the land of Sardinia on the 25th;
steering along the eastern side to the north, came to
an anchor in the Bay of Cagliari on the 27th.
Watered the fleet.   On the 4th of March, weighed
anchor and stood out to sea; saw Mount Tauro, off
the Gulf of Palma; stood in for the Gulf, and anchored at the entrance.

Came into the fleet, a cartel, with the captain and
crew of the Raven brig, which had been wrecked on
the enemy's coast, near Cadiz.   Weighed anchor,
and made several fruitless attempts to beat to the
N. W.   Beat up as high as Palma, and at five, p. m.
anchored again in the Gulf.   Arrived on the 12th,

the Active and Phœbe frigates, with intelligence of the French fleet being at anchor in Toulon.

Arrangements were made on the 15th, for the exchange of Sir Richard Strachan, and Captain Pulteney Malcolm, of the Renown. On the 16th, Captain Malcolm took the command of the Donegal, and Sir Richard Strachan of the Renown, who took her departure for England.

We were joined by the Amazon on the 24th, having taken a valuable prize; proceeded to Palma Bay, to clear transports under convoy of the Ambuscade, with Admiral Louis on board. Signal was made on the 2nd of April, to prepare letters for England, and for passengers to repair on board the Bittern sloop. The Seahorse brought intelligence of the enemy's fleet being at sea; we dispatched several frigates in pursuit, for information.

Weighed anchor on the 15th, steering for Palermo: received an account of the enemy, consisting of twelve sail of the line, two frigates, &c. steering west. Gained further information of the enemy having passed the Straits of Gibraltar, joined by a Spanish squadron; standing off and on the African shore, occasionally stretching over to the Spanish coast. We shaped our course for Tetuan Bay, on the 2nd of May; sent boats to water. We were not allowed any intercourse with the Moors, not being permitted to go beyond the beach.

A Moor of distinction came from the town, attended by four guards mounted, to prevent the lower class of people associating with the seamen. The appearance of the Moors was imposing. The country around the beach fertile, especially the valleys. The town and fortress of Tetuan are four miles from the Bay, upon the ascent of a hill, and occupy a considerable space of ground. The Moors were distant and reserved, and would not supply us with provisions of any kind. We sailed on the 5th, with an easterly wind, steering for Gibraltar, and came to an anchor in the Bay at four, p. m. Joined the fleet, and lay-to for intelligence, on the 6th. Proceeded through the Gut; made Cape St. Vincent on the 9th; anchored in Lagos Bay; employed in clearing the transports, to complete the fleet.

Lagos Bay is situated between Cape St. Vincent and the east coast of the kingdom of Portugal. The town was concealed from us by some projecting land. The country afforded a delightful prospect, being in high cultivation, and well inhabited. Signal to send letters on board the Wasp, for England.

We weighed anchor on the 11th; and at four, p. m. fell in with the Queen and Dragon, and forty-two transports, with 4,500 troops on board, from England, on a secret expedition; at seven, parted company from them. Signal to steer S. S. W., a course for the West Indies, and on the 14th made the island of Madeira. We had ten sail of the line, including one three-decker and three frigates; running nine knots an hour. Nothing particular occurred in our passage to Barbadoes, excepting hearing of the enemy having been seen steering to the southward, supposed for Martinique, with sixteen sail of the line, besides frigates.

We anchored in Carlisle Bay, on the 4th of June; at twelve, fired a royal salute, in honour of the King's birth-day. Joined by Admiral Cochrane in the Northumberland, and Spartiate. At six, p. m. took 1,500 troops on board the respective ships in the fleet, to act as circumstances might require. The soldiers were from the 15th, 96th, and 4th West India, under the command of General Sir William Myers, destined for Trinidad, to dispossess the enemy of that island, as we understood they had taken it.

We weighed anchor and steered for Trinidad : gained intelligence, on the 6th, of the enemy being at that island, with a considerable number of troops. At one, p. m. made the island of Tobago; the look-out frigate made signal of strange ships a-head, taken for the enemy; prepared for battle, neared them, and discovered them to be a convoy of mer-chantmen. At five, p. m. came abreast the fort, which saluted the Admiral. This part of the island is well cultivated, and diversified with a number of dwellings and plantations; the principal town is situated at some distance from this command.

On the 7th we made Trinidad, which resembles Tobago; but the whole island was covered with a thick vapour, the tops of the mountains being com-pletely obscured. This thick atmosphere renders the island very unhealthy to Europeans; the exhalation was so strong and dense, that I could respire with difficulty; and the land appeared to be covered with smoke.

As we passed a small fort on the coast, we observed some plantations on fire, from which we concluded the enemy had possession of the island. At five, p. m. came to an anchor in the Gulf of Paria, near the mouth of the river Orinoco, and found the island in possession of the English, and no enemy to be seen; sent into port for intelligence.

We shaped our course for Grenada on the 8th, vexed, tantalized, and perplexed. At twelve, brought to in St. George's Bay; it bore the appearance of fertility. Joined by the Jason and Emma frigates. The Bay is very capacious, and capable of containing a large fleet with safety. The town is built in a low situation, surrounded by high lands, which make it unhealthy.

Grenada surpasses all the islands I have seen in the West Indies, in point of culture and variety, being beautifully interspersed with hills and vales. After receiving the Governor's salute, and returning it, we made sail for Antigua. Passed Montserrat, and others, on the 10th; and on the 12th, anchored in St. John's Bay, Antigua. Saluted the Governor. Got intelligence of a convoy of fourteen sail having been captured by the enemy, who passed the island, steering north.

We sailed from Antigua at one, p. m. steering N. E.

having been informed that the enemy's fleet had taken that course, being three days sail a-head of us. Received orders to put the troops on board transports, and two frigates, in order to their return to Barbadoes; our detachment consisted of the 15th foot. Fell in with an American, and purchased forty-two bullocks for the fleet.

We altered our course occasionally, until we made the western islands, on the 14th of July; then took a fresh departure, and shaped our course for Cape St. Vincent, which we made on the 19th; spoke the Colossus, and a squadron under the command of Admiral Collingwood, stationed off Cadiz ; anchored in Gibraltar Bay, and completed our provisions to four months.

From the time of our departure from Cape St. Vincent, till our arrival at Trinidad, and from thence to Europe again, there had not elapsed more than two months and five days; a tolerably quick passage, including touching at several islands.

We were now employed in taking in stores, and proceeded to sea on the 22nd, steering our course for Tetuan Bay, on the African coast. Arrived on the 23rd, and commenced watering. We procured a boat, and went up to Tetuan, situated about ten miles from the Bay. We landed at a custom house, on the banks of the river, the name of which I could not learn, and then took horses to convey us to the town; my horse belonged to a Turkish soldier, for the hire of which I gave him a dollar. The saddles

E

are the worst contrived I ever saw; a piece of iron rises on the pommel, at least a foot ; a mountain of the same substance on the after part, and the stirrups like shovels.

My horse was richly caparisoned, the saddle ornamented in grand style; notwithstanding all these gay trappings, I was obliged to dismount often, to adjust my tackle, which threw me into the rear of the cavalcade two miles. I was not without apprehensions, as the Moors have frequently attempted to disarm officers when alone; however, after having cut a few capers on the road, choked with dust and scorched with heat, I arrived at Tetuan. At a distance it appears a handsome and well-built place, entirely surrounded by a wall, but when you enter it, you are annoyed by the most offensive effluvia. The streets are a continuation of passages, and covert ways. I am not surprised at the plague visiting it often.

We went to the Consul's residence, where we were regaled with eggs, fruit, and cordials. The soldier who conducted the party to the town, would not permit us to roam about at large, but attended us, like criminals, to the place from whence we came. Thus ended my peregrinations on the continent of Africa. The trade of this place is monopolized by the Jews, who are much oppressed by the Moors. The flocks and herds are numerous, and generally in good condition. The fleet received upwards of 200 of them, which proved a seasonable supply, after experiencing so many privations.

Signal to weigh anchor and put to sea, on the 24th; fell in with and spoke the Colossus, in passing through the Straits; proceeded on the 25th to the westward of Cadiz, after having been in search of the invisible foe, from January till July, repeatedly hearing of them, and at one period, we believe, were nearly up with them, just before we made Barbadoes, but were deceived by false information, and they thus eluded our pursuit. Our hopes are centred in Lord Nelson, and he will yet lead us to victory. We have this moment been apprised of the enemy; they were seen the latter end of last month, consisting of nineteen sail of the line.

Now hope rises again like the tide, and if we should be so fortunate as to fall in with them, and I survive the conflict, through the mercy of God, I hope to behold England once more, before the end of the year.

I received thirty-three dollars, on my arrival at Gibraltar, for a Dutch prize, taken two years ago. We have another in litigation, at Malta, which, if she be condemned, will give me about £12; but the grand question is, the Spanish prizes, the two frigates, the produce of which is lodged in the treasury.

After cruising about until the 11th of August, we steered for Cape Clear, on the coast of Ireland; discovered a sail, the Superb being sent in chase, brought her to; the Admiral altered his course, and on the 15th, saw the grand fleet a-head, joined com-

pany, making in all thirty-three sail of the line.   No
one can conceive the magnificence of this sight !

The Victory and Superb sailed for England on
the 16th, with Lord Nelson, to our great regret. We
gained information, that the enemy's fleet had arrived
at Ferrol, consisting of twenty-two sail of the line;
they had been engaged by Sir Robert Calder, with
fifteen sail of the line, and he had captured two
ships, one of eighty guns, and one of seventy-four.

Signal for our squadron to join the Prince of
Wales, ninety-eight guns, Sir Robert Calder ; we
made sail from the fleet, with nineteen sail of the
line ; we observed on the 20th, a frigate in pursuit
of us, firing guns, she informed us of the enemy
having sailed from Ferrol, consisting of twenty-eight
sail of the line, and five frigates, steering N. W. by W.
made all sail after them ; signal to prepare for battle ;
steering for Vigo ; stood in for the land on the 23rd ;
lay-to, and reconnoitred Vigo Bay.   Obtained information on the 24th, of the French fleet being off
Cape Espartel, near Lisbon ; made sail in that direction.   On the 25th, a man-of-war brig hove in
sight, firing guns, and sent a boat on board the
Admiral, from which we gained information of the
combined fleets of France and Spain having put
into Cadiz, and captured five sail of merchantmen,
under convoy of the Halcyon frigate, which escaped
only by the means of her sweeps.

The Blanche frigate, Captain Mudge, unfortu-

nately got among the enemy's fleet, taking them for
a convoy, and was engaged by four of them. After
gallantly fighting thirty minutes, she struck, and was
burnt to the water's edge. Two of the enemy's corvettes were afterwards taken by the Goliah, attempting to get into Ferrol.

We heard the firing of guns a-head of the fleet, on
the 27th, weathered Cape St. Vincent, bending our
course towards Cape St. Marc, expecting to meet
with Admiral Collingwood's squadron. We fell in
with it on the 29th, with eight sail of the line, and
three frigates, making twenty-seven sail of the line;
steering for Cadiz. We left Admiral Sir Richard
Bickerton at Gibraltar, in a dangerous state of illness.
Arrived off Cadiz on the 30th, five sail of the line detached to cruise in shore, under Admiral Louis, including the Donegal; parted from the fleet at five, p. m.

Stood in towards the land on the 31st; saw the
combined fleets, quietly at anchor. Obtained a better
view of them September the 1st; counted thirty-
three sail of the line, and six frigates. Observed
three admirals' flags, one at the main, two at the fore,
and one at the mizen. The remainder of the fleet
lay up at Carracas, to the eastward of Cadiz.

This city is built upon an island, communicating
with the main, by a bridge. Cruising off and on,
until September the 10th, when at ten, a.m. seven
sail were discovered, signal to chase, at eleven came
up with them, they were six transports, and one

man-of-war brig, from Gibraltar, laden with wine and spirits, for the fleet.

Signal made on the 11th to join Admiral Colling-wood, occasionally reconnoitring, but no movement was made by this tremendous force. We longed to exchange our broadsides with them. Our country must have been informed of the strength and mag-nitude of the combined fleets, ere this. We are anxious to close in battle with this leviathan-like force, and entertain little doubt as to the result; all is ardour and expectation, notwithstanding the an-ticipated bloody conflict.

After cruising for some days, our spirits were con-siderably raised on the 28th, by the arrival of the Victory, with our gallant chief Lord Nelson, accom-panied by the Thunderer and Ajax. The Euryalus arrived the same day.

On the 29th, we again reconnoitred the enemy, and on October the 1st, stood off Cadiz to rejoin the fleet; communicated with the Commander-in-chief, and on the 3rd, were detached with five sail of the line; arrived the Defiance, and on the 7th, the Naiad and Amphion, from England; at one, p. m. the Royal Sovereign appeared to leeward; arrived on the 9th, the Belleisle and the Renommé.

The Admiral shifted his flag to the Royal Sove-reign; joined on the 13th, the Agamemnon, L'Aima-ble, and Africaine; received intelligence of the Rochefort squadron having captured the convoy of

L'Aimable; sailed the Prince of Wales, for England, with Admiral Sir Robert Calder.   14th, wind N.W. strong breezes.   15th, variable ; light breezes on the 16th ; made all sail on the 17th.

Here closes the journal of my dear brother, continued to the 17th of October, 1805, within nine days of his lamented death.

The following letter, (and the last he wrote to England,) was addressed to his parents, off Cadiz, in which it appears he had communicated with his brother Robert, who was then embarked on a distant expedition.   This letter arrived in England on the 13th of November, 1805, when, alas! the dutiful son —the affectionate brother—the gallant officer—was no more.   His remains were interred by the enemy, on the Spanish shore, with his fellow-sufferers.

H. M. ship Donegal, off Cadiz,
Oct. 12, 1805.

As I have yet no prospect of seeing my best and beloved parents, for some time, I must solace myself with the hope, that when that period arrives, it will afford me ample compensation for every past anxiety and disappointment.

In my last letter, I informed you of the Donegal being attached to the advanced squadron, close in Cadiz.   Since Lord Nelson has returned, and resumed the command, we have been recalled to the fleet, which has been reinforced from England, and expect more ships daily, so that our force in these seas will be very formidable.

We heard that the enemy had orders to sail on the 25th of September, but the French admiral refused, prudently conceiving himself unequal to contend with us at this juncture. Although the affair of Ferrol has rather discomposed the public mind, I have no hesitation in declaring, that the result of a second attack will be both glorious and honourable for my country and the service ; my confidence is founded upon the ardour and eagerness evinced by every individual under his lordship's command, so much is he respected and loved.

For some time I have felt somewhat depressed, but believe it was nothing more than the vapours, arising from a want of variety ; Nelson's arrival, however, dispelled all gloomy thoughts, and re-established cheerfulness in my mind. I now endeavour, as far as my nature will admit, to exclude every idea that might tend to excite a murmur, and trust to Providence for the issue of all things.

My health, thank God, is tolerable, and I think I have my portion of happiness ; although I could, without the least inconvenience, enjoy it in a much superior degree, in the society of my dear and beloved friends: but at a crisis like this, surrounded by foes and dangers, it would be inglorious in the extreme to think of quietness and repose.

Even you, my dear father,* whose age demands a respite from the toils of war, despise the quiet of domestic life, by engaging in the service of your country. God will reward your paternal and patriotic zeal and affection.

I wrote to my brother Robert during our short stay in the channel, (only two days,) after our return from the West Indies. I have yet received no answer, which I can only attribute to his not having received my letter, as I think he had sailed from Spithead before it arrived in England.

Sometimes I fancy myself deserted by all the world, every ship brings letters to all except myself. I wrote to my brother to procure me a flute, to beguile a few tedious hours, as I could not procure one throughout the garrison of Gibraltar when there. I learn from the papers, that the Diadem is gone to the Cape of Good Hope; God grant my dear brother a safe return.

I am inclined to think an attack is meditated on Cadiz, troops are expected to co-operate with the navy. I catch the flying rumours as they pass, glad to avail myself of anything to employ my thoughts. I expect you will see a brother officer, whose friends live near you; as he is a particular friend of mine, I am sure you will pay him every attention.

I was near being ordered home, by late regula-

* Then in his sixty-first year, and an efficient private in the Staffordshire Yeomanry.

tions of the Admiralty, having reduced the number of officers in line-of-battle ships; but as we have no captain of marines on board, I shall not be allowed to quit. I should be sorry to leave this station as long as there is the smallest chance of an action; therefore I endeavour to content myself under all circumstances, and I am certain these resolutions will not be disapproved of by my dear father.

Though my efforts will be small, as an individual, yet my will is good. I am attached to my king and country,—inducements sufficient to make any inconveniences sit light and easy, and even the greatest hardships tolerable. I only wish to hear more frequently from you; it is now six months since I have received any tidings, and I begin to grow uneasy at your silence.

If I had gone to head-quarters, as a first lieutenant, I should have been ordered to embark in a frigate, and probably gone abroad again immediately. It is with reluctance that I finish my letter, but my paper will not allow me to be more communicative. My prayers and blessings for your eternal happiness, are daily offered to heaven for you all, by your

Ever affectionate Son,

JOHN F——,

First Lieutenant, R. M.

The following letter from Lieutenant Macmillan,* R. M. communicated the particulars of the death of Lieutenant John F——, to his father.

H. M. ship Donegal, off Cadiz, Nov. 1, 1805.

SIR,

It is a happy and fortunate circumstance, that notwithstanding all the misfortunes and afflictions it frequently pleases heaven to visit mankind with, there is ever some source of consolation left, particularly when we have the misfortune to lose a beloved friend or relative; and from no source can we derive more, than from the contemplation of their virtuous conduct while living, which must insure their perfect happiness in a future and a better state.

These reflections, Sir, will I hope, in some measure, alleviate the grief, which I fear you will too sensibly feel, when I communicate to you the painful and melancholy tidings of the death of your truly-beloved and much-lamented son; who, with many others, fell a sacrifice to their humane exertions, in endeavouring to procure assistance for their fellow-sufferers in distress.

Although it was our misfortune not to share in the honours of the late glorious action, (Trafalgar,) yet we arrived time enough to take possession of El Rayo, a Spanish three-decker, 112 guns, which we found at anchor, having lost her masts the preceding night.

* For the fate of this unfortunate officer, see a subsequent page.

Your son, with a party of marines, was sent on board her on the 24th of October, when it came on to blow a heavy gale from the S.W.; and on the morning of the 26th she parted her cables, and we had the mortification to see her run on shore near St. Lucar, without being able to render her any assistance. Your son requested to be sent on shore in the first boat, conceiving from his knowledge of the French language, he might be able to induce the Spaniards to send off boats to save the people on the wreck: but, alas! when he had nearly approached the beach, the surf was so high that it upset the boat, and out of twenty-six, only four persons reached the shore in safety.

The Spaniards, actuated by the noblest sentiments of humanity, attended on the beach, rendering every possible assistance to the survivors, and interring the bodies of the unfortunate sufferers.

In performing the painful and distressing task, which has devolved on me, of acquainting you of the loss of a dear and beloved son, I feel considerable alleviation in having the opportunity of expressing the sentiments of esteem and regard, which I shall ever entertain of his character; at the same time, I feel myself inadequate to do it that justice which it so truly merits. His mild and amiable manners have endeared his memory to all who intimately knew him, and left behind a lasting impression of the most sincere regret for his untimely fate.

In thus giving you the sentiments of myself

and messmates on this sad event, believe me, Sir, they are not the common eulogiums, which are generally bestowed on these occasions, but the real and heart-felt feelings of us all.   That you may bear with fortitude and resignation this trying and severe stroke, is the fervent wish of, Sir,

Your most obedient humble servant,
WILLIAM MACMILLAN,
First Lieutenant, R. M.

Copy of a letter from Pulteney Malcolm, Esq. Captain of His Majesty's ship Donegal, after his return from the West Indies.

H. M. ship Donegal, Portsmouth,
May 6th, 1806.

SIR,

Mr. Macmillan will write you particulars respecting the effects of your late excellent brother, whose melancholy fate was most sincerely regretted by every one in the Donegal, and by no one more than myself.

I never knew a more promising young man, his manners were most engaging, and his conduct in the hour of danger, would have done honour to a veteran.   If you will apply to Mr. Welsford, secretary to the Patriotic Fund, at Lloyd's Coffee House, you will receive the reward which that noble

institution gives to those who have lost their relatives in the service of their country.

I beg you to accept my best thanks for your con-
gratulations on our late success, (Sir John Duckworth's victory in the West Indies,) and remain,

Dear Sir,

Your's truly,

PULTENEY MALCOLM.*

To Capt. F.——

———

VOTE OF THE PATRIOTIC FUND.

Patriotic Fund, Lloyd's,
21st May, 1806.

SIR,

I am favoured with your letter of the 18th instant, together with Colonel Madan's and Mr. Mott's
certificates, which are perfectly regular and satisfactory; and I have to request you would be so
good as to draw for £100, (being the sum the committee have voted) at three days sight, on Sir Fran-
cis Baring, Bart., chairman of the P. F. Committee,
at Lloyd's, which shall be duly honoured.

I am, Sir,

Your most obedient humble servant,

J. P. WELSFORD, Secretary.

To Capt. F.——

* Admiral Sir Pulteney Malcolm, K. C. B.

My brother's sword, sash, gorget, and breast-plate, were carefully forwarded to England, as honourable testimonies of his active and faithful service to his king and country, and are still pre-served as memorials of his departed worth.

He had not heard of the death of his favourite brother, who died, January the 16th, 1805, at Ches-ter. He was an artist, and some time a fellow pupil under Mr. Glover, the landscape painter, with the late Henry Salt, Esq. consul-general in Egypt.

CHAPTER VI.

Commencing the services of Lieutenant Robert F——.

My youngest brother, Robert F——, was appointed an ensign in June 1803, in the second battalion of the S—— militia, commanded by Colonel E——, and was, until the summer of 1804, quartered at Newcastle-upon-Tyne, when an order arrived to encamp the regiment with a small brigade under the command of the Hon. Brigadier-General, G——. We occupied the same tent in this encampment, which was between Cullercoats and Whitley, in Northumberland. He evinced considerable military talent, and was desirous of entering the regular service.

I was fortunate enough, through the kindness of our family patrons, to succeed in procuring him a second lieutenancy, in the Chatham division of royal marines, about August 1804.

He was appointed to a frigate, intended to cruise off the Spanish coast, but his destination was altered, and he embarked on board the Diadem, sixty-four guns, commanded by Sir Home Popham, in

December 1804, and proceeded to join the fleet off Brest.   The following letter, written on his return to England, commences his journal of services, which he regularly continued.

H. M. ship Diadem, Spithead,
March 20th, 1805.

We are just arrived from a cruise off Brest, having been at sea three weeks.   We sailed again in a few days, hearing that the French fleet was at sea, consisting of twenty-four sail of the line.   Our orders were communicated by telegraph, to unmoor, and proceed to sea, with every line-of-battle ship.

It was so unexpected, that we left our captain behind.   We felt anxious to fall in with the enemy, and had some hopes of doing so, this evening, April the 6th.   After cruising some time, off and on Brest, we returned into port, and anchored, on May the 4th.

We experienced some danger in passing through the Needles; the wind shifted suddenly, and we were in danger of going upon the rocks; a frigate coming through with us, struck, and some difficulty was encountered in getting her afloat.

I remember my eldest brother describing his passage through the Needles, on his voyage to the West Indies, with a leading wind, and blowing fresh; the awful sensation, caused by the death-like silence of the troops on board—the terrific aspect of the per-

F

pendicular rocks—the velocity with which the vessel shot through into the Channel, accompanied and heightened by the reflection, that a few planks only were between them and eternity.

On the 20th of May we weighed anchor, and stood out to sea again, with the Channel fleet; not a little harassed by the enemy, for they would not leave the protection of their batteries. They would sometimes make a feint of coming out, but when we attempted to near them, put back again. On Tuesday last, we alarmed them in good earnest ; the admiral signalized to form order of battle, and led the fleet, consisting of thirty-two sail of the line, twelve of which were three-deckers, so close into Brest, that the French could count every ship singly. The British colours floating in the wind, proudly bidding defiance, ports open, matches lighted, our hearts true to the honour of old England. What a fine and glorious sight ! An Englishman might well be proud of this tremendous force. Our spirits were high, our hearts panting for a trial of strength, but nothing could move the enemy.

Their signals were flying all the time, announcing our force. We observed a fine old monastery near the beach, and could discern the French soldiers exercise, very plainly. After cruising in vain, for some weeks, we returned to Spithead, to prepare for a long and distant expedition.

August the 8th.—I should have answered your letter sooner, but was in hopes, by postponing a little, to have sent you information of our future course, but am still in the dark; the secret is not unravelled, nor will it be, till we get out from the land. You will readily conceive, with what anxiety we look forward towards our future proceedings. Sir Home Popham advises every officer to stay by the Diadem, as our cruise may be profitable; however, I shall not say much, for fear of disappointments, as it is impossible to foresee what may happen in the course of events.

Last week we received half a million of specie, and as we have baggage on board for General Fox, expect to touch at Gibraltar. The wind has just now veered round, signal is made for weighing anchor, and a gun has fired for every officer to repair on board. We expect to sail in a few hours. I shall not be able to hear of my dear friends, for some time, but shall never omit any favourable opportunity of writing. I intend keeping a journal of our transactions; we are now under weigh, and leaving the harbour.

August the 27th, Cork harbour.—We sailed from England not knowing our destination, but when we fairly got to sea Sir Home Popham ordered the ship's course to be shaped for Cork. Our expedition is still very secret, but it is surmised we are destined to attack the Cape of Good Hope. We found here, near 9,000 troops embarked under our charge, in the transports, and expect to sail to-morrow, if the wind permit.

We have now eighty ships with troops, under the command of Lieutenant-General Sir David Baird, who says we must prepare for some smart fighting. It is intended to land about 400 marines; and I have the promise of being appointed their adjutant, whilst on shore, which will increase my pay considerably. I shall send you an account of our services, if I sur-- vive; but if I fall, hope to meet my fate like a soldier, and that when put to the trial I shall resign my life as readily in defence of my king and country, as any officer in the service.

On our passage from Portsmouth to Cork, we were becalmed off Weymouth, and had the gratification of seeing our most gracious Sovereign, who came to look at the Diadem. We received him with a royal salute; he had a green shade over his eyes. After a little detention, we parted company, and proceeded on our voyage. A gun has just fired, for the fleet to proceed to sea.

October the 1st.—Funchal Roads, Madeira. We arrived safe here, with the whole of our convoy, on Sunday last, so far on our way to the scene of active service. We have just been one month on our passage from Cork, having had but indifferent weather. We shall remain here only while we can take in a supply of water, as we shall be a long time before we touch at a port again. I almost feel some attachment to this place, as two of my brothers have been here before.

I look forward to the day when we shall land,

with anxious expectation, for of our success I do not feel the least doubt.   I am happy to inform you that I have this day received my appointment as adjutant to the sea-battalion, to consist of near 1,000 marines and seamen, in the expedition to be commanded by Captain King, R. N., and therefore have not a little to do.   For this month past I have had Dundas by my side, and manœuvre a wooden regiment, every day.   I feel flattered by the appointment of Sir Home Popham, as I am nearly the junior second lieutenant, R. M. in the fleet.

I have visited a convent this morning, and passed two hours very agreeably, accompanied by a brother officer, chatting with the nuns at the grating.   Our convoy now consists of 120 sail.   The signal is just made to proceed on our voyage.

CHAPTER VII.

Capture of the Cape of Good Hope.

CAPE of Good Hope, January 18th, 1806.—It is with infinite pleasure that I resume my pen, to give you a narrative of our proceedings since leaving Madeira, of our arrival here against this place, and subsequently of its capture.   I have not time to state the circumstances so clearly as I could wish, as the ship which is under sailing orders for England, is about taking her departure.

I am this moment come on board, with the sea-battalion, after a severe and fatiguing service of ten days, in the course of which we had a long march up to the knees in sand, and very little to eat or drink during the whole time.   I now proceed to give you a few particulars.

I have added some sketches, (rough indeed,) numbered 1 and 2; they are done very ill, as I was obliged to sketch them on the back of my letter, and daub them over in haste.

On the 1st of September, we sailed from Cork, with the expedition, and arrived at Madeira on the

23rd ; after watering and taking in stores, we sailed from Funchal Roads, October the 3rd, with a favourable breeze, which in a fortnight carried us into the trade winds, running about 160 miles a day. November the 4th, we arrived at Brazil, South America, and anchored off St. Salvador.

On our passage here, we encountered a heavy gale, and had the misfortune to lose two of our convoy, the King George, transport, and the Britannia, East Indiaman. This latter, including dollars she had on board, was worth £300,000. The place where they were lost, is a small island called the Roches, just perceptible above the surface of the water, and when it blows fresh, the sea washes over it. The night being very dark, the King George struck upon the rocks, and was soon dashed in pieces; fortunately for the crew, the island was not quite covered by the sea, it not being high water, this enabled some of them to crawl along the rocks to the island, and they were all taken off next day ; the poor creatures were in a most deplorable state.

The Britannia also struck, she got off again, but unfortunately went down immediately afterwards. Some of the convoy saw her firing guns of distress, just before she sunk, and boats were immediately hoisted out, in time to save all the crew, except three ; one of which was Brigadier-General York, who, in attempting to save himself by swimming, was thrown with such violence against the side of the ship, that he sunk, and was seen no more. Another was a private artillery-man, who jumped overboard, with the intention of rendering assistance to the general, but the poor fellow, unhappily shared the same fate. The third was a seaman, who refused to quit the ship, saying, he had lived poor, and he would be d——d if he would not die rich. He went below, where the dollars were stowed, filled his shirt bosom, and came upon deck, shouting huzza ! till the ship was nearly under water. He then took off his hat, gave three cheers, and went down with her.

The country about St. Salvador, is very beautiful. We made an excursion thirty or forty miles up, and were much gratified. Tigers are found in great numbers upon the hills, which make it somewhat hazardous travelling without fire-arms.

We received a visit from the governor, and were much amused by the economy of his excellency. After waiting some time, boats were observed approaching the ship, from the shore; the accommodation ropes were in readiness ; a person without stockings ascended, and came on board. The sailors, without ceremony, put him on one side, to make way for the expected governor. We were anxiously awaiting him, when, behold, our stockingless visitor sat down very deliberately, and put on a pair of silk stockings ; he was then announced as the Governor of St. Salvador. Some apology was necessary, for the want of politeness in our tars, who were quizzing him all the time.

We paid his excellency a visit of ceremony on shore, and were received with militiary honours by the Portuguese soldiers, who paid very respectful attention to our commanders. We were amused by observing that their cartouche boxes, instead of containing ammunition, were filled with a sort of soft pudding, which we call at sea stir-a-bout, and their wooden spoons were sticking out. Their appearance did not give us a favourable opinion of their discipline. We remained at St. Salvador to refit, and take in fresh water.

December the 3rd.—We sailed with a fair wind, going down the trades at two, or two and a half degrees a day.

January the 6th, 1806.—The day being clear, we saw the coast of Africa, lying right a-head, about twenty leagues from us, and from the appearance of the land, supposed it to be the Cape of Good Hope. However, in a few hours, our suppositions were realized, which put us all in high spirits. On the 4th, we were close under the Cape, with all our force, and the troops impatient to land. We now made preparations for our debarkation, fired guns, and hoisted English colours; a broad hint to the enemy of our errand, which was quickly taken, for the town appeared in great confusion. We saw a party of cavalry, riding in various directions.

As soon as we were close enough in, the General and Commodore went in a boat to reconnoitre the place, where they intended to disembark the troops. Accordingly at daylight, the first or Highland brigade, consisting of the 71st, 72nd, and 93rd regiments, were ready in the boats, but unfortunately it came on to blow fresh, causing a tremendous surf, which rendered it utterly impossible for the troops to land, without the loss of many lives, the boats were consequently obliged to pull in again to the ships, not a little disconcerted.

In the morning of the 6th of January, a very heavy surf still running, created a good deal of anxiety on the part of the commanders, but abating a little towards evening, the General was determined at all events to attempt another landing, further down the bay, at a place called Lospord's Bay, which was effected, but not without some difficulty, owing to the wind still blowing fresh.

The Sketch, No. 1, represents it. Forty-one privates of the 93rd regiment were lost in the surf. The 72nd regiment was first put on shore, and it behaved nobly. Whilst our brave comrades were landing, we observed a party of the enemy's cavalry and riflemen advance from behind one of the hills, near the beach, and commence a smart fire upon them; but as soon as the Highlanders got sight of the enemy, they rapidly advanced, opened a fire upon them, which did much execution, and they speedily retreated.

During this affair, the remainder of the Highland brigade had disembarked, formed, and commenced their march ; we soon lost sight of them behind one of the hills. A cannonading commenced, but without material loss on either side, for the enemy retreated rapidly, except a few stragglers, who were made prisoners.

They informed us that their main body, consisting of about five thousand men, including Hottentots, was encamped behind the mountains, six or seven miles off, and intended to give us battle next evening. We were disembarking all that evening, until the middle of the next day, January the 7th ; an order then came from the General for the marine battalion, with some artillery, to re-embark, and land higher up the bay, to cut off the enemy's retreat. Accordingly we did so, and landed at the appointed place, which the Sketch, No. 2, represents.

It is astonishing to me, how we did land through such a tremendous surf, for this was the very place where the first brigade attempted to do so on the 5th, and were obliged to return on board. Our men were so eager to disembark, that it must have been a terrible sea indeed, that could have stopped them. The nearest point we could get to the shore, was forty or fifty yards, so that we were obliged to wade that distance, up to the middle, before we could reach it. I was completely ducked, for in getting out of the boat, a sea came, and dashed me over head, and I thought I should have been obliged to swim for it, but another wave set me on my legs again ; I then took to my heels, and ran till I got safely beyond the reach of the sea.   To my great annoyance, I found an excellent pistol spoiled, which I had slung in my belt, and all my ammunition rendered useless.   Several of our men experienced the same, which was an unpleasant circumstance in the face of an enemy.

The Diadem, Leda frigate, and gun-brig, covered our landing ; and just as we were leaving the boats, some of the enemy advanced down the hill, towards us, but the gun-brig opened a fire of grape shot among them, killed two, and the rest retreated. Another part of the enemy, during our debarkation, attempted to get a piece of cannon upon an eminence, but a well-directed fire from our ships completely baffled the attempts; so effectually had the squadron covered our landing.   As soon as we had formed, and our piece of artlllery was properly manned, drawn by our sailors, we advanced up the hill, ex- pecting to find the enemy there, but to our disap- pointment they had vanished.

We now observed a part of the Dutch army at some distance to our right, but could not make out if it was advancing or retreating; however, we commenced firing with our artillery upon a large building, which was situated at some distance in our front, and where we supposed some of the ene- my's cavalry to be concealed, as we saw them gallop in that direction.   After we had advanced some

LANDING THE SEA BATTALION.

76

distance, part of our own army appeared upon a hill to the left of it.

We immediately halted, and General Sir David Baird came riding up to us, apparently in high spirits, saying, " The day will soon be our own." He then ordered us to join the brigade in sight, (which proved to be the second, consisting of the twenty-fourth, fifty-ninth, and eighty-third regiments,) till further orders.

The Dutch force, that we saw on our right, proved to be a part of the army commanded by the governor, General Jansens, which had just been defeated by our second brigade, but was beginning to rally again, till he saw our force appear on the hill before mentioned : this caused him to pause a little, as he perceived we had recently landed. He was eventually determined to retreat, by a discharge of grape shot from the ships which had protected our landing, and which threw him into some confusion, so that he faced about and retreated up the country, in order to encamp.

After we had remained with the second brigade an hour or two, the General ordered us to join the Highland brigade, which had been in pursuit of the other part of the Dutch army, further up the country. Accordingly we moved forwards, and after a fatiguing pursuit of about an hour and a half, up to the knees in sand, we arrived at a sort of plain, at the foot of some mountains, where we joined the Highland brigade. We found that the enemy had retreated over the mountains, and General Ferguson, who commanded the Highland brigade, intended that we should lie on our arms all night in our present position. He had information that the Dutch general intended to surprise us during the night. A brother officer, and four or five marines, went a little distance from us, to fill their canteens with water: two Dutch officers rode towards them and fired, and afterwards retreated. In the dead of the night, just as the moon began to appear above the mountains, the enemy annoyed us by an independent firing, which continued for some time, but did us little or no injury. We were at our posts, and ready for the attack.

General Ferguson, his staff, and part of the artillery, were upon two small hills on the left; the Highland regiments on a kind of plain in the centre, and the sea battalion, with some artillery, occupied the hills to the right.

The light companies of the different regiments were in front, as the advanced guard. The hill that I was upon, was on the left of the two hills on the right, and where we had two pieces of cannon. The enemy had mounted riflemen, who dismounted when going to fire, taking aim from their horses' backs, then remounted and scampered off, so that it was impossible to lay hold of them, and they were excellent shots.

We felt the cold very severely during the night, and had nothing to lie upon but the bare sands.   A

strong easterly wind was blowing, as cold as ever I
felt it in England in the winter, and I had neither
great coat nor provisions; for what I did bring on
shore in my haversack, (which was a little bread and
meat,) was spoiled in landing, which was the case
with most of our men.

After the capitulation of General Jansens, we
marched to Rist Battery, on the 9th of January,
where we remained for some time. As this settlement
is now safely in our possession, we have returned on
board our respective ships. I expect to share between
two and three hundred pounds for this capture.

We took a French frigate, of forty-eight guns,
under the following circumstances. She ran into
Table Bay, being deceived by the Dutch ensign
flying on the flag-staff of the forts and ships, which
was on our parts a ruse de guerre. When she came
alongside of us, we hauled down the Dutch colours
and hoisted the English ensign, opened our ports,
showed our broadside, and ordered her to strike.
She lowered her colours, and I was directed by Sir
Home Popham to take possession of her, with a
party of marines.

As soon as I got on board, I saw a number of
English officers and soldiers, belonging to the 2nd
or Queen's, and the 54th regiments of foot. The
joy they expressed on our appearance I am unable
to describe. One of the officers came and shook me
by the hand, and burst into tears, he was so overjoyed: the poor soldiers were in such a state of feel-

ing, that they appeared ready to jump overboard.
Poor fellows! they had been prisoners between
seven and eight weeks, and during the greatest part
of that time had been confined below. A number
of them had died for want of air.

We now began to bring upon deck the poor sufferers who were confined below. Some of them
were so ill, from their long restraint from liberty,
that they expired as soon as they were exposed to
the air.

After the hurry was a little over, of course I was
anxious to know how they came to be taken, and
where. I was informed by one of the officers, that
they had been at Gibraltar four years, and were returning to England, not a little overjoyed at the
prospect of seeing their native land again.

When they made the British Channel, they fell in
with the French squadron, commanded by Admiral
Willaumez, consisting of eight sail of the line, and
this captured frigate, called La Voluntaire, forty-
eight guns. The French fleet chased, and soon after
took them, removed the prisoners on board this
frigate, and afterwards burnt their ship. They were
kept some time on board the French Admiral before their removal to the frigate, where they remained till we took possession of her.

When I first went on board, the French marine
officer presented me with three swords; one of
which I returned to him; another I gave to the Hon.
Lieut. Percy, (a son of Lord Beverley's, who after-

wards took the prize to England); the third was an Arabian scimitar, which I kept myself.

We had not the good fortune to fall in with the French fleet. We received information, that Admiral Linois, in the Marengo, eighty guns, and La Belle Poule frigate, was on his passage to France, from the Isle of France, with the spoils of several years of successful cruising in the Indian seas.

The Commodore placed a number of men under my command, to be trained to the use of rifles; and the light company of the seventy-first regiment was also embarked on board us. Our ship was but sixty-four guns, the Marengo eighty; but, with a select number of rifle shots, we deemed ourselves equal to the encounter, should we fall in with her; and relying on the tried courage of our men, were confident of success.

We put to sea, cruising in her track for some time, but to our great disappointment she eluded our vigilance. I am often led to think of our dear family fire-side; and how inexpressibly joyful will be the meeting, if it should please Almighty God ever to permit me to visit my native land.

CHAPTER VIII.

Conquest of Buenos Ayres, and reconquest by the Spaniards.

APRIL 12th, 1806.—We sail this evening for South America. The squadron consists of the Diadem, sixty-four guns (flag-ship); Raisonnable, sixty-four; Diomede, fifty; Leda frigate, forty-eight; and the Narcissus, thirty-two. We take the seventy-first regiment with us, commanded by Lieutenant-Colonel Pack.* Our destination is the Rio de la Plata. We calculate upon making considerable prize money, if we succeed in our attempt. It is arranged at present, if we make the land in the day-time, to stand off and on till night, then run in, and if we make good our landing, to storm the town.

The Commodore is informed by a Frenchman, now on board, (who goes with us to point out where the public money is deposited,) that the treasure is considerable. With the seamen and marines, including the seventy-first regiment, we shall land about 1800 or 2000 men. All the seamen are to be

---

* Lieutenant-General Sir D. Pack—since dead.

clothed in red, in order to deceive the Spaniards, with regard to the strength of our force. We calculate upon being opposed to about 3000 Spaniards, also to encounter a battery of seventy-three guns. Their troops are not the best disciplined in the world, which will insure us success : you may be assured that we will do our best. We are now under weigh.

St. Helena, April 19.—We sailed from the Cape on the 12th, and it is with great pleasure I embrace this opportunity of writing to my dear friends once more before we reach the place of our destination, South America. We did not intend to touch here, but last Sunday week we experienced a heavy gale, in which we parted from one of our ships with troops on board, and have some apprehension of her having foundered in the gale; for when it abated no tidings could be obtained of the ship.

The troops that we take from this island embark to-morrow, the greater part artillery. We hope to sail on Thursday, and calculate upon an eighteen or twenty days passage to the place of our proposed attack. I am reappointed as adjutant to the sea-battalion, which will consist of about 800 men, and sincerely hope that we shall have a better opportunity of distinguishing ourselves than we had at the Cape of Good Hope; the object of our enterprise is to cripple the pecuniary resources of Spain. The signal is made to repair on board; the Commodore and General are now embarking.

l have this moment heard of the melancholy death of my poor brother John, off the Spanish coast; words cannot express the excess of my feelings— poor dear fellow! He is happier than we who are left behind, in this world of trouble and sorrow. He lost his life nobly, in the cause of humanity, in his endeavours to rescue a conquered foe from a watery grave. There is some consolation that he died in the service of his country. The melancholy news was brought by a ship, which arrived just before we sailed from St. Helena.

Here there is a suspension of my brother's papers, as Buenos Ayres was recaptured on the 12th of August, 1806, when Major-General Beresford, and the British force, remained prisoners, contrary to good faith; Liniers having violated the capitulation.

Copy of a letter from Major Le Blanc,* seventy-first regiment, after his arrival in England from Buenos Ayres, respecting Lieut. Robert F——.

New Bridge Street, Blackfriars,
London, March 11, 1807.

Sir,

I feel very happy to give you every satisfaction in my power relative to your brother. I left him at Buenos Ayres well, on the 12th of August, 1806; he is not killed, or wounded, but like every one else, (myself excepted,) a prisoner of war.

* Colonel Le Blanc.

By every account we have since had, they are well treated, and remain at Buenos Ayres. I have reason to hope by this time they are retaken, and are safe with their countrymen. Your letter was forwarded to me in the country by my uncle, Sir Simon Le Blanc, or it should have been answered on Saturday.

I have the honour to be,
Sir, your obedient servant,
HENRY LE BLANC.

To Captain F———.

Copy of a letter from Lewis P. Madden, Esq. lieutenant, R. M., secretary to Sir Home Popham.

SIR,
I am desired by Sir Home Popham to acknowledge the receipt of your letter respecting your brother, Lieutenant Robert F———, as a friend and brother officer of his, who served with him at the capture of Buenos Ayres; but from the situation to which I was appointed, fortunately escaped being made a prisoner, by its reconquest.

I feel happy in replying to your inquiries, and trust it may be satisfactory. General Beresford, in a letter written four months after the recapture, states, that the officers were all well and in good health; they were treated very well by the Spaniards. There can be but little doubt, both Monte Video and Buenos Ayres must fall into our hands, and I think the officers will be immediately exchanged, or given up; most probably, one of the articles of capitulation will be directed to this head, as Sir Home Popham pressed it strongly, prior to his leaving South America.

In answer to the latter part of your letter, Sir Home directs me to express his entire satisfaction with, and approbation of, Lieutenant F——'s conduct during the time he served under his command.

I hope that you may shortly receive some good accounts from the quarter where he is, although it is impossible to say exactly the place he was sent to, but I think to Lucan, a village about sixty miles from Buenos Ayres.

> I am, Sir,
> Your very humble servant,
> LEWIS P. MADDEN.

As the Spaniards would not fulfil the terms of the capitulation, General Beresford and Lieut.-Colonel Pack effected their escape from South America, in March, 1807. General Beresford was so kind as to reply to my inquiries, as follows :—

London, June 10, 1807.

SIR,

In answer to your letter, I have the pleasure to inform you, that in February last, your brother was well, being at a place about twenty-five leagues from Buenos Ayres; and I have little doubt that before this time he is with the British army, or certainly will be ere long.

I remain, Sir,

Your very humble servant,

W. C. BERESFORD.

To Captain F——.

Nothing was heard of the captives for many months, and our anxiety was increased by various rumours of assassinations. We were at length agreeably surprised by hearing of them, through the escape of Major Tolley and Lieutenant Adamson, seventy-first regiment, who published the following paragraph in the Courier newspaper, after their arrival in England.

Colonia del Sacramento, Rio de la Plata,
June 27, 1807.

SIR,

Having effected my escape from the interior of South America, I take the liberty of informing you, that I left Lieutenant Ballinghall in good health and spirits, on the 26th of May, at the College of St. Ignatius, valley of Callimuchita, twenty leagues to the S.W. of Cordova, and about 150 to the N.W. of Buenos Ayres.

As I am not acquainted with the different addresses of the gentlemen of your corps, who are prisoners in this country, might I take the liberty to request that you will have the goodness to inform their friends, that I left the following gentlemen

along with my friend, your brother, viz. Captains
Mackenzie and Gillespie; Lieutenants F——, Lan-
del, Forbes, Pilchard, and Pollock.

They were quartered, at that time, along with the
officers of the seventy-first regiment, at a large farm-
house in the neighbourhood, with permission to
keep horses, and visit each other whenever they
pleased; four or five gentlemen were generally in
the same farm-house.

I think I may venture to say, that we shall have
the power of liberating our brother officers in a very
few weeks, as Buenos Ayres must fall immediately.

I have the honour to be, &c.

P. ADAMSON,
Lieutenant, seventy-first foot.

P. S. July 24.—Our attack has proved unfortunate,
but all the prisoners are to be liberated.

To Lieut.-Colonel Ballinghall,
    Royal Marines.

General Whitelock made an unsuccessful attack
upon Buenos Ayres, July 10, 1807. All the prisoners
were to be reciprocally given up, on condition that the
British troops evacuated the Rio de la Plata in two
months, and did not serve against South America
until their arrival in Europe.

This failure was caused by the misconduct of the
commander-in-chief, who, on his arrival in England,
was tried by a general court-martial, sentenced to be

cashiered, and rendered incapable of ever serving His Majesty again.

Lieutenant F—— arrived in Staffordshire, in January, 1808. The following is his journal of the proceedings of the expedition.

We arrived at the mouth of the Rio de la Plata, on June 12, 1807, with the squadron, under Commodore Sir Home Popham, consisting of the Diadem, 64 guns; Diomede, 50; Narcissus and Leda frigates, and Encounter gun-brig; including six transports, with the troops, under the command of Major-General Beresford.

As it was difficult to gain intelligence as to the most assailable points of the enemy's possessions in the river Plate, Sir Home Popham and General Beresford judged it expedient to defer for a day or two landing the force, and to leave it to the ultimate decision of a council of war, which was accordingly held on board the Diadem.

The result was, that we should proceed up the river with the small vessels and transports, leaving the large ships of the squadron to blockade the port of Monte Video. The Commodore then shifted his flag into the Narcissus, and collected the transports, having on board the seventy-first regiment, royal marines, two companies of the St. Helena infantry, and a detachment of royal artillery.

We made sail up the river, but were frequently obliged to anchor, on account of foul winds, and the strong tides, which were continually running against us.   The mouth of the river is upwards of 150 miles wide; and in approaching Buenos Ayres, the navigation became extremely difficult, and dangerous to strangers.   On the night of the 22nd of June, we were much alarmed on board the Narcissus, by her striking on a bank, called the ' Chico.'   She remained in this dangerous situation, till the next night, and most likely would have been lost, had it not been for the exertions of Lieutenant Talbot, of the Encounter gun-brig, who ran alongside, and lightened her by taking out some of her main-deck guns, by which means she floated, and was got off without sustaining any material damage.

We arrived off Buenos Ayres on the 25th, near Quilmes, about fifteen miles from the city.   Here General Beresford deemed it prudent to land.   We now observed that the Spaniards were collecting in great numbers at a small villiage, called Reduction, situated upon an eminence, a short distance from the beach, and upon our appearance, commenced firing alarm guns.   About four o'clock, p. m. we began to disembark the troops, which we accomplished by midnight, without any material accident, though we had a heavy surf to wade through, up to the middle.

Our force was safely landed, amounting to about 1,500 men, consisting of the different corps before named.   We lay upon our arms the remainder of the

LANDING AT QUILMES.

night, at the foot of a hill upon which the Spaniards were posted, keeping large fires burning in their front till daylight.

The night being very dark, very strict precautionary orders were issued by the General to the officers, to visit the outposts frequently, in order to keep the men upon the alert, and to prevent a surprise from the enemy's cavalry. Just before daylight we had a false alarm, which arose from our advanced pickets firing upon a drove of wild horses, supposing it to be the advance of cavalry coming down upon us.

The Spaniards lay so near us, that we had every reason to expect a charge from their cavalry, and had they fired upon us, they might have done execution. June the 26th. At daylight we saw the enemy in line in our front, consisting chiefly of cavalry, stationed on an eminence, with a morass before them. About eight o'clock we began to advance in two columns, with the artillery in the centre. After arriving within half gun-shot, we halted and formed line, expecting to receive a charge, the St. Helena infantry remaining a little in the rear, as a reserve.

We had not taken up our new position long, before the enemy opened a fire of shot and shells upon us, which passed over our heads, the guns not being sufficiently depressed. The amount of the opposing force, from what our General could learn, might be about 3000, including a column of infantry, with eight pieces of cannon, which we saw advancing on

the right of their line.   Upon observing this movement, General Beresford determined to attack them
without delay, and gave orders for the whole to advance, which was promptly and cheerfully obeyed ;
first taking off our hats, and giving three cheers, the
bagpipes of the seventy-first Highlanders striking up
at the same time.

We had not proceeded far, before we got entan-
gled in the morass, which the enemy perceiving,
opened a smart fire upon us.   Captain Le Blanc, of
the seventy-first, unfortunately lost his leg, and un-
derwent immediate amputation on the field.   We
also had several men killed or wounded ; and what
added to our difficulties at this moment was, that
our guns stuck so fast in the morass, that we could
not bring one to bear upon the enemy.   With some
exertion we cleared this impediment, and continued
to advance at double-quick time, till we arrived tolerably near ; when the enemy thought proper to retreat with the utmost precipitation, after receiving
two or three volleys of musketry, as well as a brisk
cannonading from two brass fieldpieces, which were
fortunately so much to the left of our line, that they
avoided the morass, and were enabled to gain the
heights in time to fire upon the Spaniards as they
retreated.

We were now in possession of the eminence, and
of six brass guns, left by the enemy ; who were so
inconsistent in their evolutions, that they left two of
them loaded, from which we gave them a well-

directed fire. We can only account for the trifling loss we sustained, by the inexperience of the enemy in the management of their guns, which they generally elevated too much.

The Spaniards retreated to the Baraccas, a small branch of the river Plate, which we had to cross. The General expected to meet with a stout resistance here, as he believed the enemy would destroy the bridge to prevent our crossing. Finding the pursuit useless, we halted a few hours to refresh, and then proceeded on our march towards the city.

About dark we approached the Baraccas, and observed a large fire, which we suspected to be the bridge burning. An order was now given for three companies to advance, with two fieldpieces, to endeavour to secure the bridge; but on their arrival it was found burning, and totally impassable.

Advanced pickets were immediately thrown out, along the banks of the river, to observe the enemy's motions; reconnoitering parties were likewise sent, for the purpose of discovering a place where we might cross, which, in the opinion of Captain Kennett, of the royal engineers, was not practicable at that time. Nothing remained but to force the passage, which the General determined to attempt the next morning at break of day. During the night little occurred, except that the enemy, observing the pickets relieving, opened a fire upon them, supposing them to be our main body; their fire was ineffectual, and served only to show us their position.

June 27th.—A little before break of day, our advanced pickets were ordered to retire, and as soon as daylight appeared, we observed that the enemy had taken up a position along the banks of the river, lining it for a considerable distance. Finding that our advanced posts had retired, they began to beat their drums, and shout for joy, considering this as some indication of success. However, they were soon undeceived.

The General gave orders for the whole of the troops to advance, and line the banks of the river. Our artillery at the same time opened a well-directed fire, accompanied with musketry, which was carried on briskly on both sides for more than an hour. During this time we forced a passage over, by laying planks from one vessel to another; the enemy again retreating.

A short time after this was effected, we were preparing to advance, when a flag of truce was observed. Terms of capitulation were offered, with a request to be allowed two hours longer. This our General refused; replying, that if the city did not surrender in half an hour, he would storm it. We were then within a mile and a half from it. After waiting a short time, another flag of truce arrived, agreeing to our terms.

Immediately upon this, the gates were opened to us, and our gallant little army marched triumphantly into the city, with drums beating and colours flying. We were received by the bishop and the clergy in their robes, and by the civil authorities of the place. Thus were we at last in possession of the city of Buenos Ayres, containing 70,000 inhabitants, captured by our small force, through the skill and perseverance of our commander.

June 28.—This morning British colours were hoisted on the castle, and a salute of twenty-one guns fired, which was answered by the Commodore in the Narcissus, and by the transports.

We expect to remain here nutil reinforcements come out from England, and then for more active service, as it is impossible with our small force to do much at present. The prize-money will be considerable, as the Narcissus, which takes the despatches, carries to England 1,086,000 dollars, equal to thirty tons of silver. The whole capture amounts to about 3,500,000 dollars, including Peruvian bark, various articles of merchandize, &c. Assassinations are very frequent.

For the size and situation of this city, few in Europe are constructed on a more regular plan, or better calculated for defence against a storm, as every house in itself is a fortification; the top of each being flat, with a kind of breastwork, with loopholes, so that persons might fire from them without being observed. It is situated on the south side of the Rio de la Plata, 200 miles from the entrance, and is about four miles and a half in length, and three in breadth. It is built in squares, twenty-five of which it has in length, and eighteen in breadth; each con-

taining eight very large and commodious houses,
and each having a large court in the centre.

The streets are also very regular, forming right
angles, and almost all of an equal size. It has
many churches and a cathedral, the whole richly
adorned with gold and silver, and containing very
good paintings. There is one university, several
monasteries and convents, a foundling hospital, and
a charity house, which is kept by a society of friars
called Barbones. There is one very large square,
where they have the Cabildo, or common council
house; near which is the market house. The Vice-
roy's palace is within the castle.

We remained in possession of Buenos Ayres, with
our small force, in peace and quietness, till towards
the latter end of July, when appearances began to be
a little suspicious. Frequent attempts were made to
decoy our men into the country; and about this time,
a number of the Germans belonging to the seventy-
first regiment had deserted. The General had also
been informed, that the Spaniards, observing our
force so small, (which now consisted of not more
than 1200 men,) were determined to rise, on a particular night, and surprise us.

General Beresford had bespoken a play, and the
Spaniards had fixed upon this night for the execution of their enterprise; intending to seize the General at the theatre, and the officers who attended
him; afterwards, to attack the castle. Notwithstanding this, he determined on going to the theatre,

BUENOS-AYRES FROM THE NARCISSUS.

on the night appointed, to prevent suspicion, and wished as many officers to be present as could be spared from the garrison with propriety.

When the night arrived, after giving orders for every man to be ready to turn out at a moment's notice, he went to the theatre, accompanied by a number of officers, I among the rest. During the night, we were all on our guard ; but nothing occurred, although a number of suspicious persons were about, and a great crowd at the door, on our return to the castle. When the General arrived, he found a man, who brought information that a body of Spaniards were on the march to attack us, and had arrived within three leagues. He immediately ordered out 500 men, with six guns, who advanced about half past one o'clock on the 1st of August, to meet them.

They arrived in view of the enemy about seven, and brought them to action ; after some resistance he retreated, leaving six fieldpieces in our possession. The Spaniards behaved very gallantly that morning, riding up in the face of our cannon ; and seemed determined on putting our commanding officer to death ; and would have succeeded, had it not been for a serjeant of marines, (who was his orderly that day,) and two or three of the seventy-first grenadiers, who fired and brought some of them to the ground.

One of the deserters from the seventy-first was taken prisoner during the action : he had commanded one

H

of the enemy's guns, which he stood to till the last moment. After he was taken, his former companions would have put him to death instantly, on the field, had not the officers interfered. The next day, he was tried by a court-martial, and condemned to be shot.

Towards the 8th of August, affairs wore an alarming appearance; the city was almost deserted, and, in short, we hourly expected an attack, for previously to this, the General had been informed, that a very considerable force was within three or four days march, commanded by Liniers, a Frenchman, who had lately come over with all the best Spanish troops from Monte Video.

August 9th.—This day, the deserter, who was taken on the 1st, was shot, in the presence of the garrison, pursuant to the sentence of the general court-martial. It was expected that the Spaniards would attempt a rescue; nothing particular, however, occurred, excepting that during the execution one of the sentinels was knocked down at his post. The officer of the guard came to his assistance, and was stabbed in the back very dangerously. The man who committed this outrage was immediately seized, after receiving several bayonets in his body. He evinced considerable hardihood, and even while the surgeon was dressing his wounds, seemed to set every one at defiance. We suspected that he was an emissary from the Spaniards; but he said that he would sooner suffer death than discover from whence he came, and only informed us that he was a Spaniard, and not a resident of Buenos Ayres.

August 10th.—We were informed that the enemy was now within two hours march of the city, with a train of artillery. An officer being sent to look out from one of the towers, reported that he saw a considerable force near the town, with Spanish colours flying.

Soon afterwards the Spanish General sent in his aid-de-camp, (Quintiana,) with a flag of truce. He had a great drum beating before him; this unusual mode of procession made some of us smile. He brought us a summons to surrender; demanding an immediate answer, and saying that General Liniers was ready to enter the town, at the head of a numerous army, and that he should only allow fifteen minutes. Our General returned for answer, that he should not surrender, but would meet him at the point of the bayonet.

The enemy advanced that night as far as the park, where we had a guard, consisting of a serjeant, corporal, and twenty privates, (this park is situated at the N. W. end of the town,) who, all excepting two, were put to death in a shocking manner, their bodies being cut and mangled, and afterwards thrown naked on the beach. We had several skirmishes during the night, in which Captain Ogilvie, of the artillery, and several of the men, were wounded.

August 11th.—Early this morning the enemy had

taken possession of a number of houses, from which he commenced a brisk fire of musketry, which galled our men severely. This kind of warfare was kept up the whole day without intermission. We had many killed and wounded.

August 12th.—Soon after daylight a heavy fire commenced on both sides, which was continued for some hours, when the Spaniards attempted to make a charge up one of the streets, but we gave them such a reception with our guns, loaded with grape and cannister shot, as compelled them to make a hasty retreat, with considerable loss.

Towards the middle of the day our men began to fall very fast, particularly those at the guns. They were picked off from the tops of the houses, which were occupied by the enemy, who kept up such an incessant fire of musketry, that it became impossible for the men to stand to their guns. We lost three officers almost at the same time. One was Captain Kennett, of the royal engineers; he was shot dead by the General's side.

At intervals the enemy's cavalry made several attempts to charge, but they were always repulsed with loss. However, about two o'clock the retreat was sounded, and our General ordered a flag of truce to be hoisted. His motive was, that he saw it would be only sacrificing the remainder of his men to hold out longer against an enemy six times his own number; the hospitals at this time being so full of

wounded that no more could be received; and, ulti-
mately, the Spaniards were sure to gain a victory
over us by dint of numbers.

Never shall I forget the scene which followed the
hoisting of the flag of truce, and the advantage gained over us : about 4000 ragamuffins rushed into the
square, brandishing their knives, threatening us with
destruction. The savages paid no regard to our flag
of truce, and were firing in all directions.

The whole of our little army was arranged within
the square of the castle, and all our guns double-
shotted, expecting every moment to come to close
quarters with bayonets and knives, (most of the
Spaniards being armed with the latter, which they
use with great dexterity.) Previously to this, the
General had ordered us not to allow the men to fire
a shot without his express orders, but it was with
the utmost difficulty that the General himself could
prevent it; the officers being obliged to use force to
remove the men from the guns. The poor fellows
were in the greatest state of excitement, and bitterly
lamented not being allowed to continue the action.
Some of them, with tears in their eyes, requested
most earnestly to be permitted to die with arms in
their hands. I believe a set of men were never more
ready to sacrifice their lives for their King and country, than the brave men who composed our little
army on that day.

On the approach of the Spaniards, Lieut. M———,
of the seventy-first grenadiers, was ordered out with

the picket, being first for duty.   On leaving the castle, he shook hands with us all, saying, " Are not
these fine fellows?" (alluding to his picket.) " We
will show them sport."   In about two hours he was
no more, being killed in the skirmish ; the men defended his body, and brought it in, and the next day,
after the capitulation, we buried him with military
honours.   The rascally Spaniards pelted us the
whole time we were paying our last tribute of respect
to the memory of our brave comrade, which so en-
raged our men, (though without arms,) that it was
with difficulty we could restrain them from falling
upon them.   The officers followed poor M——— to
his grave, which was truly that of a soldier, being
outside the town, for he was not allowed the rites
of sepulture in consecrated ground, being a heretic.
Here was an instance of war, stripped of all its imposing glitter.   As we laid our poor gallant friend
in his humble grave, he had the genuine tribute of
our sincere feelings.   We deeply mourned the loss
of our brave fellow-soldier.

   A grenadier of the seventy-first, during the attack,
observed a Spaniard, with a long red feather, every
now and then popping his head out of a window,
and firing upon the English, then withdrawing himself till again ready to fire.   One of this man's shots
fell very near the grenadier, who picked it up, put
it into his own musket, in addition to the charge,
and when the Spaniard appeared again from his
hiding-place, fired, and shot him dead.

Towards eight o'clock the Spanish General sent in his aid-de-camp, and finding that we were determined not to surrender at discretion, he acceded to the following terms, which our General proposed.

Article 1. The British troops to march out with all the honours of war; to be considered prisoners of war, but to be embarked as soon as possible, on board the British transports, now in the river, to be conveyed to the dominions of His Britannic Majesty.

2. The British, on their entrance into this place, having made many prisoners, who remained on their parole, and as the number of officers is much greater on one side, and of men on the other, it is agreed, that the whole shall be exchanged for the whole; the English transports returning to the place of their destination as cartels, and to be guaranteed as such, by the Spanish government, from a capture on their voyage.

3. Provisions too shall be furnished for the passage of the English troops, according to the usual custom in like cases.

4. Such wounded of the British troops as are not able to be removed on board their ships, shall remain in the hospitals at Buenos Ayres, either under the charge of the Spanish or British surgeons, at the option of the British General, and shall be furnished with every thing necessary, and on their recovery be sent to Great Britain.

5. The property of all English subjects to be respected in Buenos Ayres.

(Signed)

W. C. Beresford, Major-General.

Santiago Liniers, Capt. Spanish Navy.

August 12th, 1806.

Officers killed: Captain Kennett, royal engineers; Lieutenant Mitchell, seventy-first regiment; Ensign Lucas, ditto. Officers wounded: Captain Mackenzie, royal marines; Lieutenant Sampson, St. Helena infantry; Captain Ogilvie, royal artillery; Lieutenant Macdonald, ditto; Lieutenant-Colonel Pack, seventy-first regiment; Lieutenant Murray, ditto; Ensign Caunel, ditto. Total, three officers killed, seven wounded; two serjeants killed, seven wounded; one drummer killed; forty-three rank and file killed, and ninety-four wounded.

About four o'clock the remains of our little army marched out of the castle, with the honours of war. We hung down our heads sorrowfully, and instead of carrying our swords erect, we dropped them by our sides.

We arrived at the Cabildo, and delivered up our arms. This was the most distressing scene I ever beheld, there was scarcely a dry eye amongst us: some of the men, when they came to deliver up their muskets, broke them against the ground, cursing the day they ever took them in their hands.

Before our poor fellows were conducted to their prison, our gallant General came forward, and in an affecting manner returned them his thanks for their uniform good conduct, and expressed his happiness that every man had behaved like a hero on that day; and he hoped that they would conduct themselves with that fortitude, which became soldiers in adversity, as they had ever done in prosperity. The approbation of their commander calmed their agitation.

During the attack of this day, a number of friars were observed upon the churches, making signals to the Spaniards with small white flags. We pointed a gun now and then, and struck the cathedral, and these priests disappeared.

After we had signed our parole, I returned to the castle, with several other officers. They crowded us into a small room, placing sentries, annoying us the whole of the night, by attempting to steal what few things we had left. We were glad when daylight appeared, as it relieved us in some measure from our unpleasant situation; for we never closed our eyes during the night, expecting every moment to have a knife plunged into us.

The next morning a Spanish merchant, (at whose house I had lived when we had possession of the town,) sent his son, insisting on my coming to his house immediately. I went accordingly, and was received with the warmest welcome, being desired to consider his house my home. I met here two other English officers, the commissary-general and his assistant, who had been received in the same hospitable manner.

This was the first night for some time past that I had taken off my sword, and had lain down on a comfortable bed.

The Cabildo now put us off from day to day, with the idea that we were to be embarked on board the English transports, still lying off the town, as soon as the provisions could be got ready. However, one morning, to our great surprise, we found that the transports had sailed, having been ordered away by Liniers, who threatened to make prizes of them if they remained longer off Buenos Ayres.

We now began strongly to suspect that it was not the intention of the Spaniards to allow us to return to England, agreeably to the capitulation. A short time after our suspicions were realized, by Liniers causing a letter to be published, denying that a capitulation ever existed; we were likewise informed, confidentially, by some respectable Spaniards, who were friends to the English, that the Cabildo never intended we should leave the country from the time we were taken prisoners, but that we should be sent into the interior.

We frequently visited our poor men in prison, who were on the eve of being removed up the country. When they were informed of it, the only reply they made was, " They hoped their country would not forget them." They hung about us, and were much distressed, and parted from us in despair. A few nights before they left Buenos Ayres, some malicious persons caused an alarm to be spread, that the

English had broken out of prison. The Spanish soldiers were immediately called out, and in the confusion shot some of the inhabitants, supposing them to be our people. A servant of one of our officers was dragged out of his master's lodgings, and murdered in a most brutal manner, and his master would have shared the same fate could they have found him.

About this time I also had a narrow escape; being on a visit to a house in the same street where I lodged, the mob observed me at the window, immediately collected round the door, and insisted on my coming out. The lady of the house wished to conceal me; but as they now began to thunder at the door with great violence, and I saw no probability of their dispersing, I thought it better to make an attempt to escape to my lodgings if possible ; I therefore disguised myself as a Spaniard, passed through the mob, and reached my apartments undiscovered. This was no difficult thing to accomplish, as I had always been taken for a Spaniard, who had entered the English service, since their arrival in the Rio de la Plata. On this account I was a marked person, particularly among the lower class, who considered me as a traitor. After having been made a prisoner, I was daily in danger of being murdered ; whenever I went out, I had generally a pistol or a knife presented to my breast. They even came to my bedroom window, which fronted the street, two nights together, which obliged me to move into a back room to sleep; and I was advised to confine myself to the house.

A rascal of a Spaniard, who resided a few doors from me, publicly declared that he remembered me living at Buenos Ayres some time back, and that he went to school with me; that he knew my brother, who was an officer in the Spanish service, and was killed at Quilmes, in opposing our landing. This latter circumstance he attempted to confirm, saying, " I was in mourning for him." I wore at this time black crape round my arm, for the melancholy loss of my dear brother John at Trafalgar.

One day a cowardly assassin darted at me with a knife, but a brother officer with me warded off the blow. The villain bade me take care of myself: indeed my commanding officer was obliged to pledge himself to the authorities that I was a British officer, and had accompanied him on the expedition from England.

About October the 5th, we were ordered by the Cabildo to prepare ourselves in a few days for a journey into the interior, or as soon as a sufficient number of waggons and horses could be provided to convey us. Our men had already been sent from Buenos Ayres, and were considerably advanced on their route into the interior.

The inhabitants of this city were fond of bull-fights, which are similar to those in Old Spain, and this amusement was tolerated by the most rigid Catholics.

October 11th. This morning we were employed in packing up for our march into the country, which was to commence in the course of the day. About three o'clock, p. m. we were summoned into the square, before the Cabildo, where we found a guard of soldiers, and horses ready saddled for us. We took leave of Buenos Ayres with heavy hearts, not expecting to see it again for some time, if ever.

About dusk we arrived at the ruins of an old college, where we halted for the night, having no other bedding than bullocks' hides.

October 12th. At daylight we set out again, and arrived in the evening at the village of Luxan, about seventeen leagues from Buenos Ayres. General Beresford, and eight officers, were to remain here till further orders. The remainder were to be distributed in two small villages some leagues further on.

As soon as the waggons came up with our baggage we proceeded, and arrived on the evening of the 14th at Capillo del Señor, a much smaller village than Luxan, but more pleasantly situated. We left here Major Tolley, and twelve more officers.

October 15th. We arrived at St. Antonio de Araco, a much better and neater village than either of the two former we had passed through. Here is a very handsome church. Some large groves of peach trees, which covered several acres of ground, afforded very pleasant walks. Colonel Campbell, of the seventy-first, and the remaining officers, except four, viz. Captain Mackenzie, Mr. Lethbridge, late

secretary to Sir Home Popham, one of the assistant
commissaries-general, and myself, were to be left
here.

We had a letter of recommendation to Don Felipe
Ortorala, en sa Estania, rivero Araco; who lived
upon his estate, five leagues from St. Antonio de
Araco, where we proceeded on the 16th of October.

He received us with great hospitality, and informed us that every thing in his house was perfectly at our service, and his horses, whenever we wished
to ride out.

It is incredible the number of cattle he possessed;
I do not exactly recollect, but I know it was some
thousands.   He sold annually, (upon a moderate
computation,) 1,500 mules, which he sent to Lima.

We remained here very comfortably for some time,
our amusements consisted, chiefly, in fishing, shooting, and hunting ostriches, deer, and wild dogs. We
destroyed upwards of 500 of the latter, in four days,
they were so numerous.   These animals are so ravenous, that they will sometimes attack a man on
horseback, and frequently devour cattle.   I saw
about 100 of them attack a wild bull by surrounding
him, and they soon destroyed him.   They live in
burrows, and it is very remarkable, that no less than
five different animals occupy the same habitation,
viz : toads, rats, owls, hogs in armour, (a small animal resembling a pig,) and biseaches, which resemble a rabbit, but are three times as large.

Hunting the ostrich afforded us good sport; we

sometimes chased them for hours, but seldom or ever could come up with them, although mounted on swift horses, as they always run before the wind, spreading their wings, which act as sails on a ship; and the only method of taking them, was, to entangle their legs, by throwing the balls, which the Spaniards did with great dexterity, at the distance of eighty or one hundred yards, when in full speed.

Three of these balls, made of lead, fastened to leathern thongs, each about a yard and a half in length, tied together at the ends, one length being shorter than the other two, are swung over their heads, when they are going to throw them. With these balls they catch bullocks, horses, dogs, and even tigers, making sure of every animal they throw at.

They are also remarkably dexterous in throwing the lasso, which is a twisted leathern thong, about sixty feet long, with a small iron ring at the end, through which the other is put, so as to make a running noose, this they will throw over any part of a horse, or any other animal, with certainty, when in full gallop.

The river Parana, was within an hour's ride of our residence. We frequently went, partly to fish, and partly to enjoy the agreeable prospect, which is very striking. I took a sketch of it from an eminence, where I had an extensive view of the country, which is flat. I could observe a small vessel at some distance in the back ground, coming down the river

which winds through the valley, covered with wood,
and abounding with fruit-trees, growing wild, such
as apples, pears, peaches, &c.

This river rises in the Andes, about 500 leagues
in the interior, and falls into the Rio de la Plata.
Tigers are not uncommon here; they annoy the inhabitants, by destroying numbers of their cattle.

I was fishing one day in this river, and caught a
cat fish; it was armed with two bony substances not
unlike a saw, except that each horn had notches
or teeth, contrary ways. In order to kill it, I gave
it a kick, when it struck one of these weapons
through my boot into my foot. I forced it out, and
the excruciating pain it gave me, caused me to
faint. One of my brother officers was wounded in
the hand, and suffered much in consequence of it.

Near 3,000 Pampas (Indians) passed down the
river, about the middle of December, on their way
to Buenos Ayres, to offer their services against the
English. They were armed with spears, bows and
arrows, balls, and slings, from which they throw
stones with great exactness.

Towards the latter end of January, 1807, we were
informed of the murder of Major Ogilvie of the
royal artillery, who was one of the party left at Luxan.
He was riding one evening with Colonel Pack, of
the 71st, when they were overtaken by a Spaniard on horseback, a short distance from the village, who said he had letters from Buenos Ayres
for them, at his house, which was not very distant,

and that he would deliver them if they would accompany him thither. To this they consented; but, as night was approaching, Colonel Pack thought it prudent that they should return, beginning to suspect the man had some design, as he saw no appearance of a house.

They had scarcely turned their horses' heads, when the assassin discharged a pistol at the Major, who immediately cried out, "Colonel, I am wounded." The ball had passed below the shoulder, and had lodged in his body. The Colonel ran to support his friend, when the Spaniard ran up with a lasso, threw it, and caught the Colonel by the arm, from which he soon disentangled himself, but unfortunately had no other weapon in his hand than a small riding stick. With this he made towards the villain, who drew a sword from under his cloak, and made several cuts at him, which the Colonel received on his arm; however, he kept the murderer at bay till two men were observed approaching, when the Spaniard rode off. The poor Major had by this time fainted from loss of blood. He was carried to the village, where he afterwards expired.

A short time after this affair, a servant belonging to one of the officers of the 71st, was murdered at Capilla del Señor, as he was crossing from his master's lodgings to his own. A Spaniard caught him round the neck with a lasso, dragged him out of the village, and cut his throat from ear to ear. There were many attempts made that evening with the lasso, to ensnare

I

several of the officers; indeed, so many ill-disposed persons were lurking about, that it became dangerous for us to move out, without being well on our guard.

We sometimes thought, and not without reason, that the Cabildo was accessary to these murders, for when General Beresford applied for redress, little or no notice was taken of his application; and soon after, an order came from Buenos Ayres, for the whole of us to be removed some hundreds of miles into the interior.

The General protested against it, and said, if any thing of the kind was done, he should no longer consider himself, or any of his officers, bound by their parole.

February the 7th. We now heard of the surrender of Monte Video, to the British forces, under General Sir Samuel Auchmuty. Towards the latter end of the month, we were informed, that General Beresford and Colonel Pack had effected their escape to Monte Video, and that the remainder of the officers who were of their party at Luxan, were sent into the interior, under a strong guard. We were not at all surprised to hear of this; as the Spaniards had broken their faith with us, and had intended for some time to remove us into the interior of the country; we felt perfectly justified in attempting to escape, whenever an opportunity presented itself.

February the 26th. An order was sent to Don Felipe, from the Cabildo, to deprive us of our horses, and to keep us closely confined to the house. After remaining some time under this unpleasant restraint, about the middle of March a guard of soldiers arrived to convey us up the country.

The officer commanding the party, informed us, that we were immediately to proceed to Salto, a small fort situated on the frontiers, where the whole of the officers were to rendezvous, and to set out from thence together.

The night we left our kind host, Don Felipe, we had some idea of attemping our escape, by the way of the river Parana, but the officer of the guard, who suspected something of the kind, had planted sentries round the house.

The next morning we took our leave of Don Felipe, with the most grateful recollections of his kindness, and he seemed much hurt at the conduct of his government, in sending us further into the country. He rode with us some distance, and at parting, recommended us to the officer of the guard, requesting that he would do every thing in his power to make us comfortable during the march.

We passed through Saint Antonio de Araco, where we were joined by Colonel Campbell, and his party. The night before we left this place, we experienced the most dreadful thunder storm I ever beheld; it blew a complete hurricane, and the flashes of lightning continued visible near a minute. During this storm we were travelling upon an open extensive plain, without any shelter.

March the 26th. We arrived at Salto : it is situated on the borders of the Pampas, and is one of the frontier guards, several of which run to the westward in a line, as a defence against the Indians. There is a small fort here, with three or four swivels mounted, and a captain's guard. The Indians come down sometimes in large tribes, and annoy the Spaniards, by carrying off considerable numbers of cattle. They will occasionally attack the fort, but retreat if fired upon, having a dread of the guns, and when wounded seldom recover. They are ignorant of the use of fire-arms, supposing that they discharge themselves, and they even tremble at the sight of them, nevertheless they are a brave race of men.

The Pampas Indians are of lofty stature, but not so tall as the Patagonians ; are of an olive brown, large features, stern looks, and rather of a melancholy turn. They wear their hair, which is black and strong, turned up loose, and tied round the head.

They live chiefly upon raw flesh, preferring that of mares to horses and bullocks, and drinking their blood : they are excessively dirty in their persons, paint themselves, and seldom wash their bodies. Instead of combing their heads, they prefer encouraging the vermin, which they devour as a dainty. They are savage and intractable ; addicted to revenge. When a white man falls into their hands, they generally sacrifice him to their hatred. They are excellent horsemen ; very expert in the use of

the balls, lasso, bow, &c. and undergo hardships
with unshaken fortitude.

March 30th.—Salto. All the officers being now
collected, in order to proceed up the country, we
commenced our march, having about fifty waggons,
drawn by oxen, for the use of ourselves and servants
to sleep in, as well as for the conveyance of our
baggage.

April 2nd.—We arrived at Roxa, another of those
frontier guards. Here we halted, in order to provide ourselves with a little bread; being informed
that it was the last place at which we should be
able to procure any thing, as we were going to
enter the Pampas, where we should not see any
habitation for some time. This is generally called,
" putting to sea." After providing ourselves, we proceeded, and soon entered upon the Indian country.

It afforded but a dreary prospect to the captive;
its flatness resembling the ocean; not a tree to relieve the eye of the wanderer; cheerless as the wide
expanse of waters; an interminable wild before our
eyes, bounded only by the sky; far from our native
land, and in captivity. It was indeed a change
from prosperity to adversity. It appeared like a
dream, that we, who had so recently carried the
British arms triumphantly into the New World,
should now, alas! be prisoners, at the mercy of the
faithless Spaniards, and uncertain as to what may be
our fate.

We were already acquainted with the capture of

Maldonado, by two regiments from England, destined to reinforce us, but who arrived too late.   I
think one was the forty-seventh, under Colonel
Backhouse, the other I do not remember; also of
the capture of Monte Video, by our troops, in a
most gallant manner, by storm.   This, no doubt,
galled the Spaniards severely.

The wind blows across the Pampas plains, sometimes accompanied by thunder, lightning, and hail,
with such tremendous violence, as to destroy great
numbers of cattle.   These winds are called Pam-
peros by the Spaniards; and we experienced them
with much severity.   When the nights were dark,
we could discern the lights of the Indian fires very
distinctly.   One morning, between two and three
thousand wild horses passed us, and the Spanish
soldiers attempted to ball some of them, but they
were too swift.   These horses are highly esteemed
by them, as the finest breed in this part of South
America.   After travelling some days, our bread
began to grow short; and at times we were very
much in want of water, although we frequently
passed small rivers, but the water was brackish.
Our chief diet was beef, without salt, yet it relished
after a fatiguing march.

Our common way of cooking was, to run a stick
through the beef, and put it into the ground before
a large fire, which we always made in an evening,
after halting for the night, and sat round it.   Had a
stranger seen us then, he might have taken us for a

gang of gipsies, or banditti. Our dress was the common puncho, a sort of square horse cloth, with a hole through the middle for the head, and the corners hanging down, which formed a sort of upper garment, with a pair of pantaloons of the same stuff, and a large Spanish broad-brimmed hat.

Our beards had grown long, for we had few opportunities of shaving. I was, I believe, the only one among my captive countrymen who possessed a razor, and when we did operate it was handed round. I generally wore a Spanish knife stuck in my boot, which was useful in taking my meals, and also as a defensive weapon; we were also armed with stout truncheons.

We got information, about April 8th, of the Indians having declared war against the Spaniards, and that large bodies of the former were near us. This rendered it necessary to alter our route to the northward, and proceed by the great post road, which runs from Buenos Ayres to Cordova. This change afforded us great pleasure; for we had already remonstrated with the Spanish officer, respecting the danger and inconvenience to which we were liable, in travelling through the Indian country.

We understood that some of our men had preceded us on this road, and that the Indians proposed putting them to death. We were informed, before leaving Salto, that several had been murdered; indeed, we saw the remains of some by the road side.

April 12th. —Having now gotten into a beaten

track, called the great post road, which runs near
the river Tercero, the scene began to be a little
diversified; we passed through a number of small
villages, and now and then met with a few trees.
We continued our march along the banks of this
river, and nothing occurred to us worth observation
for some time.

April 28th.—We arrived at the village of Salta,
situated on the banks of the Tercero, about 600
miles from Buenos Ayres, and sixty from Cordova,
in which district we now were. We had a very
different prospect before us to the one we had been
accustomed to on the commencement of our journey;
instead of an extensive plain, we were in a mountainous country, extremely well wooded.

May 1st.—An order arrived from the Governor
of Cordova, for us to proceed to the valley of
Calimuchita, which lies at the foot of the mountains
we then had in view. We set out the next morning, much disappointed at not being permitted to
proceed to Cordova. The road to this valley is
very romantic : passing through the valley of Condores, which is nearly surrounded by very precipit-
ous rocks, upon the summits of which the condors
build their nests. These birds are of great size,
often measuring twelve feet from the tip of one wing
to the extremity of the other, and are very powerful
in carrying off their prey. Lions inhabit this mountainous country, but are much smaller than those of
Africa. The lama is found here ; the skin is valua-

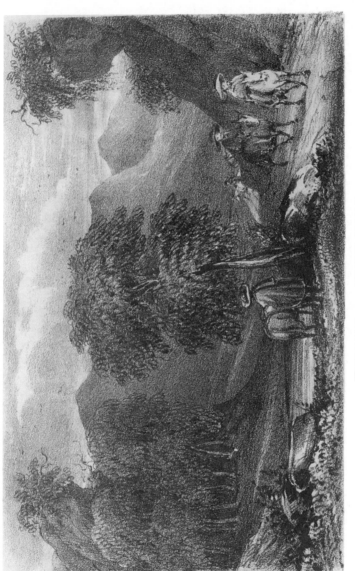

VALLEY OF CONDORES.

120

ble. We sometimes hunted these animals, but could never come up with them.

May 5th.—We arrived at a place called St. Ignacio, in the valley of Calimuchita, after a fatiguing journey of sixty days, living in carts all the time, and during the nights sleeping under the canopy of heaven, exposed to all weathers. Such is the consequence of captivity, and such is the fortune of war.

There was only one building in this place, which appeared to have been a college, belonging to the Jesuits, dedicated to St. Ignacio. Thirty officers were put into this building, and the remainder distributed in different places about the valley. We understood this place was to be our residence till further orders.

The valley is very extensive, and surrounded by high mountains, which contain mines of gold and copper, and is watered by a branch of the Tercero. We had not been here long before two of our people were murdered in a barbarous manner. A man and a woman, belonging to the seventy-first regiment, were attacked by assassins; their cries were heard by three of my brother officers and myself, and we ran to the spot, but arrived too late. We found them weltering in their blood; the poor man had about twenty wounds, inflicted by a knife; he died in a quarter of an hour; nearly the whole of his fingers were cut off the right hand, and appeared to be done by a sharp instrument, in defending himself. The poor woman was mangled in a cruel manner, and died in a few days.

We learned afterwards, that they were attacked by five or six fellows, with knives; the man defended himself and wife as long as he could, but at last fell through loss of blood. Upon hearing our approach the murderers fled. This circumstance confirmed a report we had heard, that this part of South America was infested by robbers and assassins, who, for the value of a quarter dollar, would take away the life of any person. We mutually agreed never to go out unless two or three were together, and with caution.

We remained in this vile place, shut in among the mountains, until the middle of July, when an order arrived for our removal 300 miles farther up the country. Now every reasonable person would have thought that we were quite far enough from the scene of action, for it was utterly impossible for us to hear of any thing that was going on in the River Plate, as we were already about 700 miles from Buenos Ayres.

The unfeeling Basso, head judge of the Audiencia, seemed fully determined on persecuting us to the last, for to him, and him only, were we indebted for all our privations and protracted sufferings.

According to this last order, we were to be separated, and travel in small parties, and instead of being allowed carts, we were to travel with mules.

This arrangement was made on account of our route lying through a mountainous district, scarcely passable by carts.

We now began to provide ourselves with a covering of some kind, to shelter us from the inclemency of the weather, particularly during the nights; for such were the hostile feelings of the Audiencia towards us, that nothing of the kind was to be allowed from the Spanish government, who seemed determined to treat us with the most unrelenting severity. All this was done through the inhumanity of Judge Basso.

A short time before the commencement of this journey, Major Tolley and Lieutenant Adamson, of the seventy-first, effected their escape to Monte Video. Three others made the attempt, but were not so fortunate; they were retaken a few days after they left Calimuchita, and were sent to the prison at Cordova.

Nothing very particular occurred during our residence in this valley, except that we had now and then a battle with our guard. The captain was worthless and unprincipled. Some of his soldiers had a pique against my servant: one night, after we had gone to rest, two or three of them seized him by the hair of his head, and dragged him to the stocks, which were about forty yards from the house. We heard his cries, and the whole of us immediately turned out in our shirts, armed with good sticks, attacked the guard, about thirty in number, who were armed with swords and muskets, drove them from their post, and released the man. This was a bold enterprise for unarmed prisoners, nevertheless it was the cause of their treating us with more civility in future.

July 15th.—The first party of officers set out this day, nine in number, on their march; and the second party, (in which I was to go,) was to follow in ten days or a fortnight.   We now began to despair, and to give up all thoughts of seeing England again: we hoped our country would not forget us, and fondly lingered after our homes.   We expected our destination was to the coast of Chili, where we should be lost to the world; and to be sent to the mines was certain death.

However, God, who in his mercy never forsakes his creatures, had a blessing in store for us; he had provided the means of our restoration to freedom, and very near at hand.

The first party had not been gone many days, when a man was dispatched to bring them back. A messenger had arrived from Buenos Ayres with a despatch, containing an order for the release of all the English prisoners in South America.

This order was communicated to us during the night after its arrival.   We were almost frantic with delight, congratulating each other on the prospect of revisiting our native land.

We only waited the arrival of the carts, to convey us down to Buenos Ayres, where we were ordered to appear as soon as possible.

July 23rd.—The conveyances having arrived, we set out on our journey, and arrived at Buenos Ayres on September the 5th.   During our march down the country nothing remarkable occurred.   We passed through the following places on our route, in forty-four days, viz.

Condores,	Posta de Pergamino,
Passo de Feierira,	Posta de Salto,
Frayle Muerto,	Posta de Araco,
Saladillo,	Capilla del Rosario,
Cruz Alto,	Capilla del Senor,
Esquina,	Saint Antonio de Araco,
Posta de Gallago,	Villa de Luxan,

to Buenos Ayres.   Conceive our mortification, on our first arrival, at not finding it in the possession of the English army; and we were grieved to learn, that our release from captivity did not reflect much credit on our fellow soldiers!   But why should I say so?   They were not to blame—but the chief in command.   The English soldiers will ever cheerfully follow a gallant commander to conquest.   But here! O shame! that good fine troops should have been landed, and after a severe action compelled to relinquish their enterprise, and return to Monte Video.   This place General Whitelock agreed to evacuate, on the 10th of September, provided the

whole of the British prisoners were immediately delivered up.

We called upon our friends in the city, who were
rejoiced to see us, and expressed their indignation
at the treatment we had met with from the Cabildo.
We took our leave, gratefully remembering their
kindness to us during our captivity.

September 7th.—It was now our interest to get
on board without delay, for fear of the treaty being
broken, as the time for the evacuation of South
America was nearly expired.   Accordingly, we embarked in the vessels lying in the roads, and bade an
eternal adieu to Buenos Ayres.   I was pressed by
some of my friends to remain here, offering me considerable advantages.   I must name an honourable
trait in the character of a Spanish merchant.   During the three days' attack upon the castle, I wore the
sword which I received from the French officer, on
taking possession of La Voluntaire frigate, at the
Cape.   It was a Turkish scimitar, handsomely
mounted; the hilt in the form of a cross.   When
I was made prisoner, it attracted the notice of some
Spaniards, who made repeated attempts to possess
themselves of it.   I was in daily danger of my life,
from the attacks made upon me to obtain it; but, as
it was to me an honourable trophy, I would sooner
have parted with my life than with my sword.
Finding the affair becoming serious, my Spanish
friend requested to be intrusted with it till my ex-

change or return, pledging his honour to restore it. On my release from captivity, he honourably returned me the sword, before my embarkation for Europe. Observe, that we were permitted to wear our swords, after the capitulation on the 12th of August.

September 9th.—We arrived at Monte Video, and found Admiral Murray, and the fleet, occupied in embarking the troops. We dined in the town, and had an opportunity of examining its defences.

It is built on an isthmus, regularly fortified; the houses and streets are constructed nearly upon the same plan as Buenos Ayres. It has a cathedral, besides many public buildings, and takes its name from a volcanic mountain, situated on the west side of the bay, on the top of which is a signal post.

Soon after our arrival in the River Plate, we heard, as we thought, a cannonading, and bore down in the Diadem, but found it to be an eruption of the mountain. When the British stormed this place, a Spaniard, named Manco, commanded a corps of desperadoes, or " infernals," (which last comes nearest to the Spanish word,) who neither gave nor expected quarter.

They garrisoned a redoubt, which was attacked by one of our light corps, who offered them quarter, on condition of surrendering, but they refused. It fell into our hands by storm, and most of this corps, including Manco their commander, died, in making a most desperate defence, the latter having received nearly twenty wounds from bayonets.

The ninety-fifth, (riflemen,) during the storming of this place, advanced to the breach, through a galling and destructive fire, soon dislodged the enemy, mounted it, immediately taking possession of the cathedral, and from the battlements annoyed the Spaniards so much that the place soon surrendered.

Before I take my leave of South America, a few particulars may not be out of place.

On the day of our capitulation, (12th August,) our force was diminished to about 800 men; and I am pretty well assured, that we had from ten to twelve thousand men opposed to us, of various descriptions; every house was a complete fortification, from which we were dreadfully annoyed; our ammunition was running short, and notwithstanding this difficulty our men were reluctantly forced from their guns, still anxious to support their officers.

During the assault, I had occasion to go to Captain Mackenzie for orders, when a ball struck him on the shoulder; the blood spirted out towards me. I said, "You are wounded;" he appeared unconscious of it at the time, but immediately dropped. It was a severe wound; a part of the bone, between the shoulder and elbow, was afterwards taken out, and the arm became perfectly useless. I have mentioned the circumstance, for I had a great regard for my brother officer.

We were assured soon after by Liniers, that if we had not come to terms, we should have been blown

up in the castle. Several of the sentries had reported, previous to the attack, that they heard a noise,
and felt a tremulous motion of the ground. This was
stated by one of them, but we scarcely gave him
credit. The day after our surrender, thirty barrels
of gunpowder were taken out of the mine.

The current opinion was, that if General Whitelock had succeeded in South America, the prisoners
would never have been heard of more, as our fate
would have been condemnation to the mines.

September 13th.—The whole of the British troops
being now embarked on board the transports, we got
under weigh for England, with anxious wishes to revisit our dear connexions; it is impossible to express
our feelings. Our late privations and captivity, appeared as a past dream. God had spared our lives;
we were grateful for the blessing.

Our fleet consisted of fifty sail, including the
men-of-war, under the command of Admiral Murray.
I was on board the Encounter, gun-brig, commanded by my friend, Lieutenant Talbot. We made the
island of Flores, about two hours before sunset,
bearing N. E., distance about three leagues. It
now falling a calm, a boat was manned, another
officer and myself put off for the island, for the purpose of shooting, and reached it about sunset.

This island is a barren rock, uninhabited, except
by sea-lions and sea-fowl; the latter came around us
in such numbers, that they almost darkened the air;
and we found their eggs so numerous, that we ga-

K

thered about sixty dozen in less than an hour and a
half.   As it was now getting dark, and time to go
on board, we came down to the boat for that purpose; but what was our astonishment, when we
found the gun-brig not in sight.

We had now only two alternatives, either to go in
search of the gun-brig, or remain on the island;
we chose the latter, on account of the darkness
of the night, and went in search of a place to
lie down, in order to sleep; but we found it too
cold, so amused ourselves in shooting at sea-lions,
who kept up such a continued roar, that we could
not have slept had we felt the inclination. We kept
a good fire burning all night, upon the top of the
rock, to show our companions on board that we were
still on the island, and it had the desired effect; for
on the appearance of daylight, we had the pleasure
of discerning the brig standing towards the land, and
we soon got on board. We now made all sail, in
hopes of rejoining the fleet, which had parted company from us during our detention; but all our efforts to overtake it were in vain, therefore we shaped
our course for England alone.

October 18th.—After having been at sea five
weeks, we arrived at the city of Pernambuco, on the
coast of Brazil, where we put in for fresh water. It
appears well built, the streets regular, and kept remarkably clean. The harbour is good, and sheltered by a chain of rocks, that form a complete bar
across its entrance, having a small opening for ships.

It is not calculated for large vessels; there is not
sufficient depth of water. On its left is a round
tower, mounting three guns.

About two miles from this place, there is another
town, named Olinda, situated upon a rising ground,
covered with wood ; the merchants have their country residences here. There are several nunneries,
and a cathedral. We remained here two days, and
were very civilly treated by the Governor and inhabitants.

October 21st.—We sailed on our voyage, and
passed the island of Ferrand de Norohna, about
three degrees south of the Equator, on the 24th. It
is inhabited by convicts, sent here by the Portuguese.

November 5th.—We crossed the line with a fine
breeze, an extraordinary occurrence, as calms generally prevail here. About the beginning of November, we got into a regular trade wind, which kept
with us till we got well to the northward of the
tropic of Cancer.

November 10th.—Spoke an American vessel, and
received information of our being at war with Den-
mark. 12th. Fell in with one of the convoy, but she
could give us no account of the fleet, not having
seen it for five weeks. She informed us that one of
the transports, having on board part of the seventy-
first regiment, went down at sea, after leaving the
river Plate, but happily no lives were lost.

November 20th.—Arrived off two of the western

K 2

islands, Corvo and Flores; were becalmed under them two or three days.   Flores is the largest of the two, and distant about four leagues from the former. 24th. Got a fair wind, running eight and nine knots an hour; our hopes were to see England in ten days, as our passage had been tedious hitherto; however, we lost this favourable wind, and our hopes vanished, and prognostications of a gale from the eastward were observed.

November 28th.—Came on to blow a stiff gale, which in two or three days became a perfect hurri-came, which obliged us to lie-to, under the storm stay-sail; we shipped several seas, one of which would have certainly filled the brig, had not her head been brought to it.

December 5th.—The gale began to abate, but we found ourselves drifted considerably to the south-ward, nearly 2º 30'.   12th. Fell in with one of our three-deckers, the Gibraltar, 80 guns, in the Bay of Biscay; she gave us information of our being at war with Russia and Portugal.   December 16th. De-scried the coast of England, and on the 19th, came to anchor at Spithead, after a tedious passage of ninety-eight days.   We could not learn anything of Admiral Murray's fleet.

I had now been absent three years on active ser-vice, and found my health began to be much im-paired; obtained leave of absence for two months to revisit my dear native home, and on January 1, 1808, I was once more sheltered beneath the kind and hospitable roof of my dear parents, who received me with the most heartfelt joy.

I have preserved the following letters from two valued friends, one a fellow-captive, and the other a lieutenant of the Diadem.

Cordova, June 13, 1807.

DEAR F———,

Now, my dear fellow, it is your turn, as Pollock had the first, and Murray the last; and although that was the case, do not think it was through partiality, for could the whole of my attention be taken up by you three, believe me it would be equally divided.

We have not much news, but I believe the best I can give you is, that the bearer is come to pay you. We have already received ours, amounting to sixty-one dollars, but the merchants have only received four rials per day; this hurts them much, and some of them have been to the treasurer to say, it was hard that they, who had brought merchandise into the country, should have no more; while we, who came to rob and plunder them, should receive a dollar.

D——— has taken up miniature-painting, but you know the man.   W——— and the Italian were very near entering the lists of fame; this has set the ladies' tongues a-going.   Captain B——— has joined you before this; he left us on Wednesday last.   We

naval gentry were confined to the house for upwards
of eight days, under a strong guard, incommunica-
ble.   Indeed, the first night they confined us, two
fieldpieces were placed in front of the house, with
orders to fire into the first room that made a noise ;
but Chenowith and myself remonstrated, and wrote to
the Governor, stating we were non-combatants; upon
which we had permission to reside in the town, and
be considered as merchants.

I have sent the scarlet and black silk, also the
thimbles for Anderson ; a blue puncho is not to be
got for any money.   Remember me kindly to all my
fellow-prisoners, and shall be happy to do any thing
for them here ; believe me

Very truly your's
T. A. L————.

To Lieutenant F——,
   St. Ignacio.

Mr. L—— was secretary to Sir Home Popham,
and knew my eldest brother when quartered near
Plymouth, in Devonshire.   I have inserted these
letters, to prove the kind feelings existing among
British officers on service ; it is undoubtedly a happy circumstance in our country, that the profession
of arms gives to its natives a higher tone of feeling,
and attachment to a comrade, than the service of
any other state in Europe.

Cape of Good Hope,
Oct. 20, 1807.

DEAR F——,

I was favoured with your letter of the 12th of September, a few days since. It gives me great pleasure to hear that you are all well, after the difficulties and distresses you have gone through.

Your box of clothes and writing desk I put on board the Polyphemus, 64 guns, Rear-Admiral Murray's ship, the day before I left Monte Video, with a letter to you, and a number of the captives.

Yesterday, on cleaning out the store-room, a bag of papers, belonging to Captain G——, was brought to me, which bag I have made up, and sent by this conveyance to Captain Madden, and enclosed a lottery ticket, or rather one-sixteenth, which was found among the papers. Should you know Captain G——'s address, be pleased to write to him, saying what I have done, and tender my warmest friendship and respect. For you, my friend, may you be recompensed for all your sufferings. May God bless you, send you health, wealth, and prosperity. I am, dear F——, with the sincerest friendship,

Your's truly,

D. BARTHOLOMEW,
Lieutenant, R. N.

To Lieutenant F——.

P. S. Should you not have received your desk

and box before you left Monte Video, make inquiry
on board the Polyphemus.   I delivered them myself, spoke to Captain Haywood for permission, and
he was pleased to give orders to receive them ;
and gave directions, that as soon as any of the prisoners came down the country, they should be delivered.

CHAPTER IX.

Expedition to the Scheldt.—Services in the Mediterranean, on the coasts of Spain and Portugal, until his return to England with prisoners, after the battle of Busaco.

AFTER remaining some time in Staffordshire, I was attacked by severe illness, suffering much pain in my head, attributable to the Pampero winds, of South America, and sleeping on the ground, on our march up the country.—I felt anxious to exchange my service to the line. The 85th regiment lying in cantonments near me, the adjutant wished to resign in my favour, and a mutual agreement was made, but did not succeed, owing to a misunderstanding betwen the commanding officer and the adjutant. I received the following recommendatory letter, from Captain King, R. N. who commanded the sea battalion, on shore, to which I was appointed adjutant.

London, April 8th, 1808.

DEAR SIR,

Sir Home Popham has requested me to reply to your letter, on the subject of your obtaining the

adjutancy of a regiment of the line. He would have
answered it himself, but conceived it would better
answer your purpose for me to do so, as you served
more immediately under my command in that ca-
pacity.

I am sorry for want of judgment, not to be better
able to do you justice, but as far as I could take the
liberty to give an opinion, the colonel of the regiment you mention, will be fortunate in your joining
him.

It would be presumption in me to give a decided
opinion in military matters, but this I have a right
to say, that you always performed the duty of adjutant to the marine battalion on an arduous service,
with perfect ability and unremitting attention; and
if any thing should ever throw me into the same line
of service, it would be a great relief to my mind, to
have so good and able an assistant. Wishing you
every success, I remain, dear Sir,

Yours truly,

WILLIAM KING.

To Lieutenant F——, R. M.

Lieutenant F——'s health being much amended,
he proceeded to the head quarters of his division at
Portsmouth, and continued on duty until July the
1st, 1809, when he was ordered to embark on board
the Statira frigate, thirty-eight guns, commanded
by Captain W. C. Boys, with a detachment of royal
marines, under his command, consisting of a second

PASSAGE OF THE WESTERN SCHELDT FORCED.

lieutenant, two serjeants, and fifty-six rank and file.

The Statira sailed to cruise off the French coast, to watch the movements of the enemy. After remaining in the Channel some time, she returned into port to join the expedition against Flushing. After various services on the Dutch coast during the siege, she joined a squadron of frigates in forcing a passage through the Western Scheldt.—The following letter, containing an account of the action, is from Lieutenant F———.

H. M. ship Statira, Western Scheldt,
August 21st, 1809.

It is now midnight, and my watch on deck, and as every thing seems quiet for the moment, (notwithstanding we are close to the enemy,) I embrace this opportunity, to give you an account, which I shall dispatch by a frigate which will sail early in the morning. I have enclosed a sketch of our forcing the batteries of Flushing and Cadsand, which was accomplished with little loss ; about twenty killed and wounded.

Our squadron, of ten frigates was led in gallant style, by Lord William Stuart in the Lavinia, and engaged with the batteries nearly two hours. The cannonading was tremendous, about 600 pieces of ordnance firing at the same time, which, added to the bursting of shells over us, was a magnificent, yet an awful sight.

I assure you, my sketch is very inferior to the ap-

pearance of the engagement, although it shews you
our correct position during the action. To a spec-
tator, the sight must have been imposing.

The frigates could only be distinguished at intervals, emerging from the smoke. I had the command
of six thirty-two-pounders, on the quarter-deck, with
the royal marines ; and we fired, I believe, forty
rounds out of each gun, during the two hours ; they
became so heated, that two or three of my guns dismounted, and wounded several of the men ; we
were, in consequence, obliged to reduce the quantity
of powder.

If you had seen me during the action, you would
have taken me for any thing but an officer, for I was
as black as a sweep.   In the middle of the conflict it
became so hot, that I threw off my uniform and neck-
cloth, and unbuttoned my shirt collar, consequently,
the powder had so completely blackened my shirt
and face, that had a soot bag been shaken over me,
I could not have been worse. I have scarcely been
able to use my right hand since, the skin having
been taken off four of my fingers, by the friction of
the ropes, in working the guns ; for I pulled and
hauled as well as my men, not choosing to remain
inactive, when the shot were flying about.

I have, providentially, hitherto escaped all danger,
but our labours have scarcely yet commenced.   We
are now preparing for a grand attack upon the
French fleet, which we expect, will be attempted the
day after to-morrow.   Our advanced guards, station-

ed for the night, are now engaged with some of the
enemy's detached batteries ; in short, we have con-
tinual skirmishing.

We are up the Scheldt, a short distance from
Antwerp, the enemy's fleet lying there, of which we
hope to be in possession before many days are past.
A strong chain or boom, runs across the river, from
one battery to another, which must be forced before
we can reach the enemy.

I am now trespassing upon my middle watch, in
the hope of relieving the anxiety of my dear friends,
by giving proof in black and white, of my being still
in the land of the living. We are so near, that we
can discern the enemy relieving guard; we now and
then salute with a few shot, to keep them on the
alert. I do not get more than three hours' rest out
of the twenty-four.

Flushing surrendered, on the 15th of August.
The bombardment was a terrific sight ; what with
the flashing of the guns, the bursting of shells, the
rockets flying, and the town at intervals in flames,
it was a spectacle altogether beyond my powers of
description.

After the surrender, the streets presented a mournful spectacle, the dead bodies (of men, women, and
children) not having been carried away.

A council of war was held, which decided upon
the impracticability of our passing up to Antwerp,
therefore, the plan of forcing the boom was aban-

doned, and we received orders to drop down the Scheldt.

We have lost many men by sickness, on the expedition; sixteen officers died in the fleet in one night; and we also committed to the deep, the bodies of fourteen men; indeed the Walcheren fever is making dreadful ravages. The morning before we sailed from Flushing, 1 went on shore, to take a last view of the ruins of the town. The sight was a melancholy one, scarcely a part of the place escaped the destructive effects of shot, shells, and rockets : even whole families, in their attempt to conceal themselves in cellars, were blown up by shells penetrating the earth ; for there was no place of safety. Sometimes, during the bombardment, sixteen or seventeen shells would burst in the air at one time, in the night. Farewell to the Scheldt; we are now getting under weigh for Portsmouth, and expect to sail immediately for Spain.

We anchored in the Downs on the 12th of September. You shall hear from me again, before we take our departure. Having had a wish to serve with Lord William Stuart, since I had the honour to sail with him in the squadron of frigates, up the Western Scheldt; I availed myself of the opportunity of exchanging from the Statira, to the Lavinia frigate, with the officer commanding the royal marines, and have the satisfaction of serving now under his lordship's command.

November the 15th. The Statira has sailed with a convoy for Newfoundland, and is to proceed from thence to the West Indies. The Lavinia dropped down to Spithead, to complete her stores for foreign service; we are now ready for sea, waiting only for orders.

December the 6th. Lord William Stuart arrived with sailing orders; our destination is the Mediterranean, and we proceed with the first fair wind. The Marquis and Marchioness of ———, a daughter, with several others, and a retinue of servants, embarked yesterday on board the Lavinia. The marchioness is in a delicate state of health, and a voyage to a warmer climate being recommended, the family availed themselves, on this favourable occasion, of a voyage to the Mediterranean, on board the Lavinia. A boat just going on shore enables me to say, we proceed direct to Sicily, having a quantity of specie shipped on board us; the wind is yet unfavourable. Your kindness I shall never forget, in giving up your interest to me, by requesting the approbation of the Hon. Major-General Stewart, to my exchanging my present service for the line, into his regiment, the third battalion of the ninety-fifth.

I find my health suffer from confinement on board a ship, and I shall most gladly accept the opportunity of transferring my services from the royal marines to the land forces. The wind is fair, and we are now weighing the anchor.

Copy of two letters from the Hon. Major-General Stewart, in answer to an application in favour of Lieut. Robert F——, R. M.

Sandgate, Folkstone,
Oct. 23d, 1809.

My dear Sir,

Your letter of the 22nd September, having, as I imagined, lodged with Messrs. Greenwood and Cox, who have ceased to be my agents, did not come to my hands until a considerable time after date. I ought to apologise, however, for not having replied to it sooner by a few days than I have done; but from a multiplicity of business, having an extensive district to inspect for the autumn, and not less than sixteen corps, I have scarcely had an hour at my command.

After the flattering account which you have given of your brother's services, and of his desire to enter the ninety-fifth regiment, I shall certainly, if in my power, recommend him for a second lieutenancy in my battalion, as soon as I shall have received his answer to a letter which I have this day written to him at Portsmouth.

There are at this moment only two second lieutenancies vacant in my battalion, and they are stated by the agent to be for purchase. I shall, however, make inquiry, and get one of them, if possible, transferred to one of the other battalions. When I learn more I shall not fail to give you information. If your brother has left this country for the East Indies,

it will, I suppose, be difficult to effect our object;
let me know.   Your health is, I trust, re-established.

I have the honour to be,

Dear Sir, very faithfully your's,

WILLIAM STEWART.

To Captain F———.

Sandgate,
Dec. 4, 1809.

MY DEAR SIR,

On the same day that I received your last
letter, of the 22d November, I wrote to your brother,
on board the Lavinia frigate, requesting him to send
me such a letter as should authorise me, during his
absence abroad, to act upon his wishes of entering
the ninety-fifth regiment, both towards his colonel of
marines, and the Commander-in-chief at the Horse
Guards.   I at the same time informed him, that the
two second lieutenancies in the third battalion,
ninety-fifth regiment, are for purchase, and that all
that I could do was, to say, that I would promise
him the first vacancy that should occur, or induce
one of my brother colonels to let him succeed to
one of theirs.

I have not received any answer from your brother,
and therefore fear that he has sailed.   If he has left
no letter of resignation, or letter officially expressive
of his wish to transfer his service from the marines
to the line, I know not what could be done during
his absence.   If I find, however, that I can effect it,

I shall not fail to do so ; and have this day written to General Sir Brent Spencer,* to inquire whether he can give him one of his second lieutenancies in the mean time.   When I first wrote to you about my early hope of getting your brother into my battalion, I did not know that the Commander-in-chief destined both of the second lieutenancies for purchase.

I have the honour to be, &c.

Faithfully yours,
WM. STEWART.

To Capt. F——.

Gibraltar, January 19th, 1810.—We anchored here last night, after midnight, for the purpose of repairing our rigging, which received considerable damage in the gales we experienced on our passage from England.

I am at this moment very unwell, in my cot, to which I have been confined a week; what with a pain in my head, and the motion of the ship, writing is an undertaking I am scarcely equal to ; however, I thought a few lines would be acceptable to you, as well as to my dear parents.   I had obtained a frank from the Marquis of ———— ; but we sailed so suddenly from Spithead, the wind coming round in an instant, that I was disappointed.

I attribute my illness to our beating to quarters one evening, off the Spanish coast.   The night was dark and damp; I was thinly clad, having just risen

* Died in January 1829.

from my bed.   A light being observed on our weather bow, the drum beat to arms, and to clear for
action; but the ship proved a friend.

We sailed from Spithead on the 5th January,
through the Needles.   The night before, we had a
ball and supper on board, it being the birth-night of
Lord ———— ————, Lord William's nephew.   A
sea struck us on the quarter, during a gale, and
stove in part of our stern windows.   Captain M——,
brigade major at Gibraltar, is just come on board to
see me.   I knew him at Portsmouth.   We are
weighing the anchor.

Malta, March 13th.—The word is just passed,
announcing to the ship's company an opportunity of
sending letters to England.

We remained at Sicily a fortnight; touched first
at Palermo, the residence of the royal family.   The
country is enchanting.   I took a sketch of the harbour for Lord William, also one for Lady —— ————.
It was the intention of our noble passengers to have
remained at this place, but a house was not to be
procured suitable to their rank.

Lord ————, the English minister, is living here
in great splendour.   I was invited to a ball given by
his lordship; and being informed that the royal
family would be there, Lord William gave me a
letter of introduction.   I did not anticipate much
pleasure, but felt desirous to see the Sicilian court,
and accompanied Lord —— ————, (the Marquis
of ——'s grandson,) his lordship's tutor, the family

physician, and a brother lieutenant, forming a tolerable party.

After having been there an hour or two, I began to grow tired, notwithstanding it was one of the most splendid entertainments of the kind I ever saw. There were upwards of 600 people present, including some of every European nation. It was crowded to excess, so that we had scarcely room to move. The party I went with, feeling as much fatigued as myself, would gladly have retired about twelve o'clock, but Lady ——— politely requested us to stay supper in a friendly way, observing, that she had only invited a few, and those chiefly English.

This induced us to remain; but, to confess the truth, I would rather have retired, as we did not sit down to supper till five o'clock in the morning.

The King and Queen of Naples, and royal family, were present, and walked through the rooms without any kind of ceremony. When they stood, every body did the same, facing them. This part of the ceremony we did not understand; and one or two of us were standing close to the Queen, with our backs towards her, when Lord ——— came to us, whispering, with a smile, " The Queen is close to your elbow."

I was much amused, in the early part of the evening, in walking through the different rooms, by looking at the gaming tables. One in particular attracted my attention, surrounded by princesses, duchesses, &c. belonging to the Sicilian court; they were playing high, having some thousands of dollars placed in the middle of the table. Those who were losing, every now and then were wound up to such a pitch of anger, that I expected to see it end in manual proceedings.

At supper, Lady ——— remarked, that this gambling, (a vice to which the Italians are devoted,) was very unpleasant to her; but it being a long established custom, and very general, if prohibited at her house, it would be considered a violation of good manners.

We sailed for Messina, the most considerable town on the western coast of Sicily. On passing through the Straits, the French fired upon us from their batteries; as their shot did us no damage, we did not think it worth our while to return their civilities.

One part of Messina is still in ruins, the sad memento of an earthquake, which destroyed it twenty-three years ago. The night of our arrival here, there was such a severe shock, that the inhabitants fled from their houses in great confusion, expecting destruction every moment. Our ship felt it sensibly, appearing as if she had struck upon a rock, which alarmed us very much.

Most of the Sicilians slept in the streets this night, and some took refuge in the country, not daring to remain in the town. I dined at the commissary-general's, the following day; he informed me, that when the shock was first felt, he was at table with a large party, when the candlesticks were thrown down with some violence. The company gazed at each other with astonishment for a few seconds, then guessing the cause, jumped up and ran into the street, where they found the inhabitants in the greatest consternation. It was observed, that if there had not been an eruption of Mount Etna last year, the town would certainly have been destroyed by this shock, which was more violent during the time it lasted, thirty or forty seconds, than the one which made it a heap of ruins, and continued five days, at intervals.

The Marquis did not approve of this place, as a residence for his family, we therefore proceeded to Malta, and landed them. We expect to sail with a convoy in April, if so, hope to be in England about May. The Marquis has procured the governor's house for his family, situated about five miles in the country. I have had the honour to dine there several times with my brother officers, and we have a general invitation. I experience much pleasure in his society, he is so condescending and kind. His lordship having passed much of his time in Spain, we have frequent and long conversations, about the manners, customs, &c. as well as of those of South America. I gave him my journal to read, he was pleased to observe, that it agreed well with the accounts he had himself heard from the Spaniards, who had travelled in that country.

He generally addresses me in Spanish, as I speak the language tolerably. We have had several very agreeable parties, since the health of the Marchioness has improved. She gave us a ball and supper, which was delightfully pleasant; we had also some music.

On visiting St. Paul's cave, can you imagine my dear brother, the excess of my feelings, in observing the name of our dear brother John cut in the roof, he having visited it when at Malta in the Donegal. I have cut out the piece of the rock, with the imprint of his much-loved name, and will bring it to England for you, if God spare my life.

Spithead, May the 29th, 1810. We sailed from Malta on the 7th of April; we touched at Cadiz, but did not remain long; nothing occurred of any importance during our passage to England. The service of a marine officer is now very monotonous, I am anxious for a more active life,—no prize-money to be made, and very little inducement to continue. Our future destination is very uncertain.

June the 13th. Owing to the boisterous weather we have had this day at Spithead, I did not receive your letter before the evening. I have spoken to General Elliot about getting relieved, and find that the specified time which would authorise him to disembark me from sea duty, without permission from the Admiralty, is three years; therefore, under existing circumstances, it will be highly requisite for me to apply to their lordships.

Lord William Stuart is expected from town on Saturday, when I shall forward my application through him. English officers are to be allowed to enter the Persian service, in order to introduce European tactics, it would suit me well, if they hold out promotion.

June the 23rd. Our captain is arrived, and we have received orders to proceed immediately to Plymouth ; our destination is Lisbon. I have received a letter from Mr. ——, and he informs me, that he has had some conversation with the Hon. Mrs. Stewart, and if I will write to the General, under cover to her, she will forward it, as soon as she can learn where he is ; but has every reason to suppose, that he is with Lord Wellington. It is not very unlikely but I may see him, soon after our arrival at Lisbon, I will then offer my services as a volunteer in the 95th, and carry a musket until I obtain my commission. The ship is unmoored, the boat is waiting, and I am going on board, as the sails are bent.

Plymouth Dock, July the 6th. I received your letter on our arrival here, with much pleasure, because it has relieved my anxiety. Lord William is of opinion, that the Admiralty will yet relieve me, if we do not put to sea immediately. You mention, my dear brother, the probability of my communicating with General Sir Brent Spencer, at Lisbon. If General Stewart be in Portugal, I may without any intrusion, address him.

I met an officer of the ninety-fifth, a few days ago, just returned from the Peninsula, but he could give me no account of the General. I am very anxious to hear again from you before we sail, but if I should not have that satisfaction, I shall make myself happy with the thought, that you will not forget me ; you have my interest at heart. I shall never be able to repay you, my dear brother, for the trouble and anxiety you have had on my account, but I shall not cease to remember it.

The Marquis of ———, and family, are just arrived from Malta. I am going to pay my respects to them. Our present orders are, to proceed to Lisbon, but the Admiral has also received other orders, to detain us till further instructions.

I have been taken for a Spaniard in this place, the people gaping at me with surprise, saying, "There goes the Spaniard." It amuses Lord William much. I can say, with sincerity, that my thoughts are often occupied about my dearest friends ; though actively engaged, my mind occasionally relaxes from the sterner duties of my profession, and wanders to my paternal roof. There is something solemn, nay, affecting, in pacing the quarter-deck of a man-of-war, in the night watch, when all is still.

July the 10th. Our destination is changed, and we proceed to Cadiz with a convoy; this is fortunate, particularly if your letter should precede me, addressed to the General there. I will take an early opportunity of inquiring him out, and propose to join him as a volunteer.

July the 17th. In this instance, I may with propriety make use of the old adage, Tis an ill wind that blows nobody good. It has blown excessively hard from the westward, for two or three days, which has prevented our sailing with the convoy, but has given me the inexpressible pleasure of receiving your very kind letter, of the 9th instant.

When one of the midshipmen brought it, I was shut up in my cabin, quite absorbed in reading a book I had borrowed from Lord William Stuart, which was recommended to me by the Marquis of ——, when at Malta, The Life of Valette, one of the Grand Masters of Malta, who made so gallant a defence against the Turks, when besieging the island.

I found this book so very interesting, that had it not been for the arrival of your letter, I believe I should have read myself nearly blind; however, the pleasure of again hearing from you, before quitting England, superseded every thing else, and Valette was consigned to the shelf. I assure you, my dear brother, that the satisfaction I experienced from your kind communication, was gratefully acknowledged, by the overflowings of an affectionate heart. I was much affected at your account of the melancholy death of our poor friend, J. H. W.; I feel greatly concerned for his afflicted relatives. When you write to his worthy family, pray include me in your letter of condolence.

How little dependence is to be placed on sublunary things! Yet, as you justly observe, though human life is short, all our days are numbered,—the soldier will not die on the field of battle, nor the

sick man in his bed, before his appointed time.
How much this reliance on the unsearchable wisdom
of Providence reconciles us to the most trying
events! Some may smile at the doctrine of predes-
tination, " that every bullet brings its billet," yet a
soldier or sailor under this impression is resigned to
his fate, and submits to the will of God.

As a further proof of the verity of your assertion,
I have to inform you of a circumstance that will
excite your sympathy. Poor Macmillan, (now a
captain in our corps,) the writer of that affecting
and beautiful letter respecting the death of our lamented brother John, is now an invalid in the
Royal Hospital, Plymouth, deprived of speech, and
partly of the use of his limbs; even his intellects
are at times deranged. Our surgeon, who knew
him well, had occasion to go to the Hospital on
duty, and there accidentally saw him.

Being ignorant of his unfortunate situation, he
accosted him with the salutation of an old friend,
offering his hand. The poor sufferer, with tears in
his eyes, made an attempt to return it, but alas! he
could not raise his arm, nor was he able even to tell
his sad misfortune; but with tears trickling down
his cheeks, shook his head, and gave him a look
expressive of such deep sorrow, that the sympathis-
ing doctor fancied that he himself had caught the
contagion, and felt in his turn unable to speak or
move, but stood gazing with wonder and astonishment at the altered countenance of his friend, who

but the other day was a fine active young man.   I
wish much to see him, but fear it would only add to
his distress.   He has been brought into his present
unhappy situation by a wound which he formerly
received on his head.

I have this moment received a letter from my
friend Gibson, informing me that the Lavinia will
proceed first to Cadiz with a convoy, and afterwards
to Lisbon, probably to remain some time upon that
station.   I hope this will not interfere with my
arrangements.   Communication is very frequent
with England, and I may be permitted to join the
army before an action takes place ; nothing would
give me greater satisfaction, be the consequence
what it may ; I am prepared for the worst, and hope
always to be able to meet a soldier's fate with resignation.   Your letter is arrived, enclosing the copy
of one from the Commander-in-chief, which has
proved satisfactory ; and I now trust that the Admiralty will disembark me.   We are still at anchor,
the wind continues unfavourable, and I hope to hear
from you again before we sail.

Lord William Stuart told me the other day, (by
way of compliment I suppose,) that he was glad for
his own sake that they had not relieved me, but that
he was sorry for mine ; yet he had much satisfaction
in taking me out with him again under his command.   Although he has little or no interest at this
time, I may depend upon his exertions to serve me.
His lordship is eccentric, but his character is noble

and generous; his mind rather of a melancholy and reflective turn. I frequently walk the quarter-deck with him in an evening, conversing upon the great uncertainty of happiness. There is something so manly and attractive in his deportment, that one cannot help feeling attached to him. He likewise possesses great taste, and is an excellent connoisseur in paintings, and is fond of conversing about them.

My hope of hearing again from you before leaving England is this moment vanished; the wind is now fair, and we are preparing to weigh anchor. Farewell.

Copy of a letter from His Excellency General Sir David Dundas, K. B. Commander-in-chief, &c.

Sir,

I am directed by the Commander-in-chief, to acknowledge the receipt of your letter of the 9th instant, with its enclosures, and to acquaint you, that your brother has been recommended, by Major-General the Hon. William Stewart, through Major-General Sir Brent Spencer, for a commission in the ninety-fifth regiment, for which purpose his name has been noted, but at present there is no vacancy.

I am, Sir,

Your obedient servant,

H. TORRENS.*

To Capt. F——.

* Died in 1828.

Copy of a letter from the Hon. Major-General Stewart, from Portugal.

Sardezas, near Castel Branco,
August 15th, 1810.

MY DEAR SIR,

Having received a letter from your brother a short time ago, at Lisbon, renewing his request to be admitted into the ninety-fifth regiment, and observing two vacancies in the last monthly return which has been transmitted to me, I have this day written to the agent, (the only channel of communication with the War Office, the Lieutenant-Colonel of the third battalion, ninety-fifth regiment, being in Spain,) to lay your brother's name before the Commander-in-chief, for the first of the two vacancies, if they be without purchase.

As his letter to me is with my baggage at Lisbon, I know not his Christian name; and as it is necessary that his resignation in the marines be given in, you will do well to write on both subjects to Mr. Adair, and also to forward your brother's resignation, which he informed me that he authorised you, or some one, I forget whom, to deliver for him.

In short, transact the business for your brother, and I shall be most gratified to hear of his entering the ninety-fifth regiment. He is somewhere on this station, I know not where.

I have the honour to be, faithfully yours,
WILLIAM STEWART.

To Capt F——.

Mons. Regnier is in our front. All well.

Lisbon, August 30th.—I take the earliest opportunity of transmitting you a letter that I have received from the Hon. Major-General Stewart, with one enclosed for the Hon. Admiral Berkeley, commanding on this station, to which the Lavinia is attached.

Sardezas, August 18th, 1810.

My dear Sir,

Your letter of the 14th instant was delivered to me, and I lose no time in enclosing a letter to the Hon. Admiral Berkeley, regarding his sanction to your leaving the Lavinia, and joining the ninety-fifth regiment, as a volunteer, if Lord William Stuart do not object to the same, that is, in the event of Lord Wellington acceding to a measure which is rather of a novel description.

I shall write to Lord Wellington to-morrow on the subject, and state, as your name has been notified at the War Office, for the ninety-fifth regiment, and as I have by a letter, a few days ago, to the agent of the ninety-fifth regiment, recommended you for the first vacancy in my battalion, to the Commander-in-chief, it is my wish that his lordship permit you to join the first battalion, now near Celerico; as the Lieutenant-Colonel's assent to this step must, however, be previously obtained, my letter to Lord Wellington must pass through that field officer's hands, this will cause a day or two more delay.

If the measure be acceded to by the four persons concerned, you will do well to take advantage of some detachment of the army going to head quarters; and in this case it will also be well that you previously write to Lieutenant-Colonel Beckwith, and learn the footing on which he may be inclined to receive you.

You must be aware that your services will be without pay or allowance, excepting rations at the army, until you receive a commission in the ninety-fifth regiment. Consider, therefore, whether you had not best wait on shipboard your actual appointment in the regiment; less delay will probably occur in your receiving that appointment if you do not wait, but some inconvenience may *per interim* occur. I enclose a letter to Admiral Berkeley, in which I have mentioned your wish; you will have the goodness to deliver it to the Admiral, and state your case.

I have the honour to be, dear Sir,

Your very faithful and humble servant,

WILLIAM STEWART.

To Lieut. F.——, R. M.
Lisbon Station.

Agreeably to the General's directions, I waited upon Admiral Berkeley, (Lord William Stuart having previously paved the way by calling upon him,) but judge of my disappointment, when I learnt that he had not the power to permit me to leave the Lavinia, without an order from the Admiralty. Nay, although I even requested of him to accept my resignation, as I was determined to join the army before an action took place, (which was then hourly expected, a number of waggons having been ordered up to receive the wounded in the event,) and Lord William seeing my anxiety, pressed my suit with the Admiral, offering me letters of recommendation. The Admiral again said, it was utterly impossible for him to accept my resignation, or to allow me to quit the ship under any pretence; it was as much as his commission was worth, without an order from England, or he should have been happy to have obliged General Stewart.

So you see, my dear brother, that it is out of my power to avail myself of any opportunity that may occur to my advantage, while I remain in the ship on this station: unless an authority be sent out from the Admiralty for my discharge from the Lavinia, I could not accept of a commission, if the General were to enclose me one, therefore I must rely on your kindness to settle this point for me.

I have not yet replied to his kind letter, as I am in expectation of receiving another from him, with the result of his application to Lord Wellington. I shall write to the General, to inform him that I have communicated with you, and at the same time express my disappointment at not being allowed to quit my ship.

I am going to dine with Colonel H——, of the fourteenth light dragoons, who came out with us in the Lavinia; he is an excellent draftsman, and ad-

M

mirer of paintings. I find him a very gentlemanlike man, and one who requires little ceremony; he
sketches well, and I have derived much improvement
from his instructions. He sets out for the army in
two days, and will be the bearer of a letter from me
to the General.

Lord William Stuart's kindness renders my disappointment supportable. He frequently takes me out
to dinner parties, and has given me a letter of introduction to a family of distinction, where I have a
general invitation : he has also presented me to our
Envoy, Mr. Stuart. His lordship has expended a
considerable sum in pictures, and often consults me
when he purchases. He has given me one, (having
heard me admire some parts of it,) the subject of
which is the Ark resting upon Mount Ararat; it is
an old one, in very good preservation, and its size
about five feet by four. I shall preserve it for
you.

There are two others which he is endeavouring to
purchase for me, but as the vender asks a considerable price for them, I fear my modesty will not permit me to accept of them, unless he lowers his demand. I had finished two large sketches for you,
and intended to have had them framed, but his lordship saw and admired them, so that I could not help
begging his acceptance of them.

I have no news of importance to send you, except
that the French have completed their works before
Almeida, and it is expected they will immediately

open upon it. Colonel H—— informed me this morning that our army had advanced. I have had a good deal of conversation with the Colonel and Lord William, on the subject of my quitting the marine service, and their wishes perfectly coincide with mine.

I enclose you a copy of the resignation of my commission in my present corps, the original of which I left with Patten in the adjutant's office, at Portsmouth, when I left England in January last, to be forwarded through General Elliot. As this may possibly be mislaid, I wish you to act upon the enclosure.

Colonel H—— has promised to send me news from the army, and I have engaged to forward to him any occurrence from Lisbon. I have been with him nearly the whole day, purchasing pictures, &c. Almeida has fallen into the hands of the French. Our army has not retired, as reported in the English papers. I did not mention to you in a former letter, that on my arrival from Malta, on the 29th of May last, I found a letter lying in the post-office for me, at Portsmouth, from General Stewart; the following is a copy.

Portsmouth, Jan. 4, 1810.

Sir,

Understanding that the Lavinia is still at Spithead, I shall be gratified by seeing you at the Lieutenant-Governor's any time that you may come on shore, as I shall be glad to hear that your views of entering the ninety-fifth regiment have been met by Major-General Sir Brent Spencer, of the second battalion, to whom I wrote some time ago on the subject.

I have the honour to be,
Your very faithful servant,
WILLIAM STEWART.

To Lieut. F——, R. M.

Of course I felt vexed when I found that we had only left Spithead the same day, and anchored off Yarmouth, near the Needles, from which place we did not sail till the 6th; during which time we had no communication with the shore, consequently, the General's letter and yours remained in the office till our return.

Transport ship Frances, at sea, October 1st.—I expect the receipt of this letter will occasion some surprise, on account of its being from a transport at sea; but to remove all conjecture, I must inform you, that I am now on my passage to England, and as our progress on the ocean is slow, the ship being but an indifferent sailer, I write this in the hope of some vessel passing us, homeward bound, by which means you may hear something of me, in the event of any accident happening.

I take this precaution, as I am not in a man-of-war, and not a great distance from the French coast, independent of other circumstances, which make it highly necessary. I have 270 prisoners on board, (principally French, taken at the battle of Busaco,) under my charge, and have only fifteen marines to guard them, which I conceive is a very inadequate force for this service, in the event of their rising upon me.

I am obliged to keep a sharp look out, as we are daily nearing the French coast, having no particular desire to have my throat cut. I have generally for my bedfellows a brace of loaded pistols and my sword, and the men follow my example.

The nights being very dark, I never permit more than a few upon deck at one time to breathe the fresh air, but allow them every indulgence I possibly can, as prisoners of war, having been in captivity myself. If they do not make an attempt to carry the ship into a French port, I must confess I shall consider them a set of very inoffensive fellows. From their external appearance, you would fancy them capable of undertaking any daring enterprise; they have mustachios of immense size, and you would suppose that no razor had passed over their chins for twelve months.

The evening is far advanced; we can observe a large ship on our lee-bow, but cannot make out what she is; however, I have ordered all the Frenchmen below, and as it is now bed-time, I shall wish you good night; you would perhaps smile to see me, in my nightcap, loading my pistols, and putting them to bed.

October 19th.—It is now near nineteen days since

I wished you good night, during which time we have
been tossed about with such terrible gales, that as
often as we made the coast of England, we were as
often blown out to sea again by the tempestuous
weather; and on the nights of the 12th to the 15th
instant, we were nearly driven on the rocks of Scilly.
At one time we were so close, that had the ship
missed stays, or stood on ten minutes longer, we
must have gone on the rocks; but happily for us,
she obeyed the helm.   It was blowing a heavy gale,
the sea running mountains high, and the night very
dark.   The horrors of the scene were increased by
the rain descending in torrents.

Not a night passed on this eventful duty, but I
dreamt of my native land; often thinking of your
family, seated round a comfortable fireside; but how
soon was I recalled to a sense of the miserable contrast afforded by my present situation, when a heavy
sea, every now and then breaking over the ship, made
her heel to such a degree, that it was with the greatest difficulty I could save myself from being thrown
out of my cot.

During this gale, our poor prisoners suffered
much; they were in a state of mutiny, I should
rather say frenzy, without my being able to afford
them the smallest relief, consistent with the safety of
the ship and crew.   My own armed party being so
few, were harassed to death by the severity of their
duty, and I had some difficulty in preserving subor-
dination.

I was forced to threats, and declared I would shoot the first man that flinched from his duty. Remembering, my dear brother, your early initiation of me into the prime duty of a soldier, by a short maxim, which embraces in its precepts the well-being of His Majesty's service, " To obey, and to be obeyed." This has ever been my motto, and will be as long as I have the honour to serve my country. Without attention to this, the discipline of the army could not be upheld.

On entering the Channel, we observed a man-of-war, and communicated with her. I made known my situation, and was immediately supplied with rockets and blue lights, which I was directed to use if occasion required. Thank God, we are now out of danger; the wind suddenly shifting round in our favour last night, and after a month's perilous voyage, we are coming to an anchor at Spithead. I cannot sufficiently describe my present feelings; they are like those of a man who is reprieved, after receiving sentence of death.

During one of the gales, we threw overboard several of the unfortunate Frenchmen, who had died during the passage from illness.

I have not the smallest idea, until I have seen the Admiral, how they intend disposing of me, now my ship is on a foreign station; whether I am to be discharged from the Lavinia, or to be considered as still belonging to her, till her arrival in England. She sailed two days before me, for the Western

Isles.   The Admiral at Lisbon, knowing my anxiety
to get to England, appointed me to this service,
which I am happy to say is over, through the sug-
gestions of Lord William Stuart.

The Lavinia is this moment hove in sight, and
will be at her anchorage to-morrow.

CHAPTER X.

*From his illness in Haslar Hospital, and appointment to the
ninety-fifth, to his embarkation for the Peninsula, in June,
1812.*

OCTOBER 25th, 1810.   I have delayed writing a
few days, hoping to send you information of my
being relieved from the frigate, but have not yet
been able to accomplish it.   Upon communicating
with the adjutant, I am informed that eight first
lieutenants are ordered round to Chatham, to embark on foreign service.

The Lavinia is ordered to refit here, which may
detain her a month, therefore shall not make application to be disembarked until I hear further.   I am
determined, my dear brother, to go out to Spain as
a volunteer, sooner than go to sea again; and as
Lord William Stuart resigns the Lavinia, with a
change of most of the officers, she will not be so
pleasant in future.   His lordship advises me to resign my commission in the marines, rather than go
out again.

I met an officer of the ninety-fifth yesterday, just

arrived from the Peninsula; he informed me that
Colonel Beckwith was speaking of me, and expected
me to join him as a volunteer. I wrote to the
Colonel before I left the Tagus, informing him that
such was my intention as soon as I got relieved by
the Admiralty. I have received Lord Wellington's
permission to join the first battalion, as well as that
of Colonel Beckwith.

Spithead, November 9th.—My leave came down
from the Admiralty yesterday, and they have only
allowed me a fortnight, from the 8th instant. I fear
that I shall lose a few days of this indulgence
through indisposition, for I am at present confined to
my room with a violent cold and stiff neck, accompanied with feverish symptoms.

I had determined to set out immediately, but the
surgeon of the ship advised me not to think of it, as
he apprehended a severe illness would be the consequence; I have therefore taken lodgings for a few
days, for the comfort of a good fireside, for it was
miserably cold, wet, and comfortless on board, the
whole of our cabin being knocked down, and under-
going a thorough repair.

The paintings I have brought for you are packed
up in a case, which I shall send by waggon, six in
number. The large one is a parting present from
my noble and kind commander, Lord William
Stuart,* when we separated at Lisbon. The oval
pair I bought out of a convent in Sicily, and the

* Died at Jamaica, in command of the Conquestador, 50 guns.

other three from Malta. I am vexed that they are rubbed a little on their passage, but could not avoid it; indeed I was obliged to nail them to the top of my cabin, we were so full of French prisoners. They are all ancient, and would not bear much knocking about.

I shall bring your coins myself, as well as two or three other curiosities, not of much value, nevertheless, may not be unworthy a corner in your cabinet. One is a piece of stone from St. Paul's cave, in Malta, with dear John's name cut upon it, which I have before noticed. A human bone, which a friar allowed me to take, when exploring the catacombs, from a stone coffin; also some ashes, given to me by the commissary-general, as a great curiosity; having been thrown upwards of sixty miles from Mount Etna, and fell like a shower of hail, completely darkening the air. This fall preceded the eruption.

Haslar Hospital, November 21st.—When your letter arrived, dated the 12th instant, I was removed to the hospital, consequently did not get it until the 17th. Here I am, at last, laid up by sickness, after so much active service; surrounded by calamities, and the dark side of human life. In the chapel yard of this establishment lie the remains of my dear brother Henry, who died here on the 30th of November, 1803 : the wounded men of our navy and army, who have been serving abroad,—some dying daily, others in a state of convalescence.

I was unwilling to enter this place, hoping my attack would give way to medicine, but was obliged to submit to the unpleasant alternative. My constitution is somewhat shaken by former privations, and considerable anxiety of mind. I was removed here in a sedan chair, about eight days ago, in a weak state. I have experienced the most marked attention from some of the principal families of this neighbourhood. I expect another officer will be sent on board the Lavinia to relieve me, the captain having made a demand at the Admiral's office to that effect; the ship being in a state of forwardness. I am approaching a state of convalescence, but am much reduced; my native air, and the society of my dear friends, will soon restore me to health; and I hope shortly to be again ready for service, as I am very anxious to join the army in Portugal before a general action takes place.

I have annexed a copy of Colonel Beckwith's* letter, which I replied to before I left the Tagus, informing him of the impediments I had met with, and of my not being allowed to quit the ship on a foreign station.

Camp, near Celerico,
Aug. 27th, 1810.

Sir,

Having, in compliance with the wishes of the Hon. Major-General Stewart, applied to his Excel-

---

* Major-General Sir T. Sidney Beckwith, K. C. B. colonel of the second battalion, rifle brigade.

lency Lord Wellington, to grant permission for your joining the first battalion, ninety-fifth regiment, I beg leave to acquaint you, that on receiving the sanction of the proper authorities in His Majesty's navy, his lordship has no objection to your doing so, and to your being attached to the corps as a volunteer.

I have the honour to be, Sir,

Your most obedient servant,

T. SIDNEY BECKWITH,

Lieut.-Colonel, first battalion, 95th.

To Lieutenant F———,
H. M. ship Lavinia, Tagus.

I shall send Mr. Adair a copy of this letter, and shall write to my friend Gibson.*   I am still improving in health, and if permitted to go on leave for a short time, I shall soon be stout again.

November 29th.—I am not yet relieved from the Lavinia, so tardy are they; but such is the etiquette of our service, and I must not complain.   I am now dragging on a miserable existence: this seeming inattention preys upon my mind.   I assure you, my dear brother, I feel it most sensibly, as an ungrateful return for past sufferings and service; and if I were to express my feelings ingenuously, I would prefer dying a volunteer in the brave ninety-fifth, than remain here; do not think me impatient; strange as

---

* Since dead—a private secretary at the Admiralty.

this declaration may appear, it springs from my heart.

I am informed by some of the officers of the Lavinia, (who are remarkably attentive to me, and in my sick room every day,) that she is going to the Mediterranean, to remain two or three years. I have many friends here, who are exerting themselves in my behalf : my anxiety to join General Stewart increases.

A number of the ninety-fifth riflemen are in this hospital, just arrived from the Peninsula, many of them dangerously wounded. I have been conversing with two of them this morning; one is blind from his wound, and the other not expected to live twelve hours longer, being shot through the body. His spirits are astonishing, and his voice strong. He related to me last evening an account of the action in which he received his wound, and every now and then broke out into such an enthusiastic strain, when he spoke of his comrades in the field, that I was obliged to check him, expecting every minute to be his last, and requested him not to exert himself so much.

The doctor has just paid me a visit, and informs me that my poor ninety-fifth friend is now dying, but still raving about the action of the 27th. I almost feel a wish to see him again, but there are so many around him I shall decline it. There are about 700 wounded men here, from the late skirmishing in Portugal; twenty of them died within the last three days, and were buried this morning; fifteen more are now lying dead, and many others expected in the course of the day.   The forty-third and ninety-fifth regiments have suffered most.

December 5th.—I am now considerably better, and hope to obtain leave of absence in about a fortnight, to complete my recovery.   I have been in the hospital near six weeks, and shall be allowed two months leave.

Could the gay and thoughtless take a glance at this abode of suffering and death, and hear the groans of the wounded soldiers, they must possess hearts of adamant if they did not deeply sympathise with the sufferers.   The king of terrors reigns paramount; honour appears as an empty sound; the warrior is here mortal, and returns to dust.   Notwithstanding these heart-rending scenes, under the feeling of convalescence, my desire has returned to join the army in Portugal.   I even find in this hospital, something to alleviate the melancholy thoughts attending a residence in it; a consolatory charm, which emits a ray of hope and comfort,—indeed I might say, divine comfort,—implicit faith in God.

And now, figure to yourself my present companion, a venerable clergyman, who has joined me in my sick room, and whose benevolent friendship I shall always value.   We take our social cup of tea in an evening, like two old maids; he always provides, cuts the bread and butter, and I assist to eat it. It has an air of much comfort, to see an old gentleman, with his white wig, sitting on one side of the fire, making an excellent cup of tea, while his companion, a convalescent soldier, is enjoying it on the other side. I brought some beautiful Spanish music, given me by some Portuguese ladies, who came in the Lavinia, to England.

I am just informed, that I am at last relieved from the Lavinia, and an officer has been sent on board to succeed me.

I received a letter yesterday from Mr. Adair, a copy of which I annex.

Pall Mall, London,
Nov. 30th, 1810.

SIR,

From information I have been able to procure, I have reason to believe you have been noticed for a second lieutenancy in the ninety-fifth regiment, but from the peculiar circumstances of the times, no notification has yet been made out for you. On this consideration, it appears to me, you may send in the resignation of your commission in the marines; and you will of course determine, whether it may be advisable to go to Portugal previous to a notification being made out for you, which does not strike me as absolutely necessary.

I am, Sir,
Your most obedient servant,
ALEX. ADAIR.

To Lieut. F——, R. M.

You will see, my dear brother, that this is satisfactory; yet I am desirous to be in Portugal, as I should not like to lose the chance of a general action.

———

Copy of a letter from the Hon. Major-General Stewart.

Chamusca, Nov. 23rd, 1810.

MY DEAR SIR,

Your letter of the 24th September, now by me, was put into my hands after the return of our army from a campaign in the upper part of this kingdom. Your brother and the Lavinia having left Lisbon before our return to its neighbourhood, I had it not in my power to do the only thing which can possibly satisfactorily arrange the affair of his entering the ninety-fifth regiment, I mean by a personal interview with him.

Where he is now, I could not learn at Lisbon a short time ago; but when you write to him, you will have the goodness to let him know, that the commanding officer of the third battalion, ninety-fifth regiment, at Cadiz, (Lieutenant-Colonel Barnard,) having informed me, about two months ago, that a vacancy of a second lieutenancy, without purchase, having occurred, by the death of an officer at Cadiz, I lost no time, but wrote, both to Lieutenant-Colonel Barnard, and to the agent, Mr. Adair, to give in your

N

brother's name for the vacancy to the Commander-in-chief, as you state that a friend at the Admiralty is prepared to give in his resignation (your brother's) whenever requisite.

I am in hope of hearing before long, that the affair has been arranged to the satisfaction of both of you.   I am here with General Hill's division, part of an army of 11,000 men, under his orders, which crossed the Tagus on the 18th, with a view of marching to Abrantes, and getting into the line of Massena's retreat.   We are halted here, that retreat not being so decided a case, a few days will, however, determine.

I have the honour to be,

Dear Sir, your faithful servant,

WILLIAM STEWART.

To Capt. F——.

When you write to your brother, apologize to him for my not having replied to his letter of the 31st August, from Lisbon, about Admiral Berkeley not letting him quit the Lavinia there, and volunteer with the ninety-fifth regiment.   I did not fail to give attention to its contents.

W. S.

———

Marine Barracks, Portsmouth,
Jan. 10, 1811.

I am, as you will perceive, discharged from sick quarters, but owing to the few officers here for duty, the General hesitated to forward my application for leave, but at last consented to apply for a month's leave. I am advised to wait a little, as three lieutenants are expected round from Chatham, to head the roster, for sea-duty.

I shall value very much your present of the dirk, and if I have occasion to use it, the recollection of its having been presented to me by an affectionate brother and fellow soldier, will be a sufficient stimulus before an enemy.

January 31st. Your letter I have this moment received, in a packet from our friend Gibson. I have just time to inform you of what steps I have taken, as I found I should not be able to get up to town time enough to go out with the reinforcements from Portsmouth, now waiting for a fair wind.

The regiments marched in and embarked immediately, even without refreshment. I hope to be able to join my countrymen. In short, go I must, if possible, although it will be a great trial to me to give up seeing my dear friends again; but I must plead a soldier's duty, anxious to serve his king and country; therefore I have, my dear brother, addressed the Commander-in-chief, stating my wish to go out with the reinforcements now embarking, as I have been accepted as a volunteer in the ninety-fifth by Lord Wellington. In order that you may be informed a little of the nature of my request, I send you a copy of the letter I have addressed to Sir David

Dundas, which I sent on Friday last, the 25th of January.

Marine Barracks, Portsmouth,
Jan. 25th, 1811.

SIR,

I have the honour to address your Excellency, in consequence of having had a correspondence with the Hon. Major-General Stewart, respecting my entering the third battalion, ninety-fifth regiment, of which he is Colonel, and joining the army in Portugal.

When I was at Lisbon, being desirous to join the ninety-fifth as a volunteer, I obtained, through the Hon. Major-General Stewart, the sanction of Lord Wellington to do so, as well as Lieutenant-Colonel Beckwith's; but I could not avail myself of it, in consequence of being ordered to England with a detachment of marines, to escort French prisoners.

Since my arrival in England, I understand that the Hon. Major-General Stewart has recommended me for a second lieutenancy in his battalion, become vacant by the death of an officer at Cadiz; and by a letter addressed to my brother, dated Horse Guards, 19th December, 1810, I find that your Excellency also has promised to avail yourself of the first opportunity of recommending me for a commission in that regiment. It is on this presumption that I have taken the liberty to address your Excellency, to know if I may hope for your permission to join the regiment, on actual service, with Lord Wellington.

If I be so fortunate as to obtain your Excellency's approval of my request, I shall consider myself most happy, and will immediately resign my marine commission, and hold myself in readiness to embark. Fearing, in my anxiety to go out to Portugal, I may not have conformed to the rules of office, it is necessary that I should offer an apology, but must rely on your Excellency's indulgence for pardon.

I have the honour to be,

Your Excellency's most obedient

and very humble servant,

ROBERT F————,

First Lieutenant, R. M.

To His Excellency Sir David Dundas, K. B. &c. &c. Commander-in-chief, Horse Guards, London.

As soon as I get an answer, I will inform you, without delay. The idea of addressing Sir David Dundas was suggested by our good friend Gibson, he having informed me, that officers who had been promised commissions, were actually going out to join, as if they had been gazetted, but the sanction of the Commander-in-chief is necessary to this step, such a pledge being thought sufficient for the commissions being subsequently granted, as the signature of the King followed the will of the Commander-in-chief: this is, however, I am sorry to say, too late, for the troops sailed this morning.

Copy of a letter from the Hon. Major-General
Stewart.

Chamusca, January 25th, 1811.

My Dear Sir,

I only received your letter, dated the 25th of
November, a few days ago, it having apparently been
intrusted to private hands.   I lose no time in recommending to you, to advise your brother, whose con-
tinual anxiety to enter the ninety-fifth regiment, is
highly flattering to it, to continue his service in the
marines, until a vacancy actually occur in that regiment, and which he can secure; however, he must
not be from England, as you state, that the resignation of his marine commission will not be accepted,
while he is serving abroad.

I am ignorant, at this distance, whether there are
vacancies in my battalion, and of course, know less
of the other two, but as I wrote more than once, and
long ago, both to the agent, (Mr. Adair,) and Lieutenant-Colonel Barnard at Cadiz, to secure a vacancy
for your brother, when one should occur without
purchase; I have always indulged the hope, that
matters were settled to his satisfaction by this time.
I shall take another early opportunity of renewing
my directions to these gentlemen, but in the meantime, as I perceive not that your brother will gain
his object more speedily by leaving the marines,
than if he await a vacancy in England, I think he
had better pause, before he abandons his present
commission in that service.

In the meantime, I recommend, that if your brother retain his intention of entering the ninety-fifth regiment, and care not particularly, which battalion, (no object of importance,) he lose no time in writing an official letter to each of the three commanding officers, Lieutenant-Colonels, Beckwith, Wade, and Barnard, stating his wish, requesting their protection of the same, and my recommendation, that he should address them on the subject.

Your brother pays too handsome a compliment to the regiment, in what he proposes, for him to have any scruples in thus personally addressing himself to these commanding officers. I shall send this letter to the Adjutant-General's office, and request his forwarding it to you. I feel infinite regret at your brother's indisposition, and trust that he has recovered, long before this time. I have the honour to be,

My dear Sir,
Your very faithful servant,
WILLIAM STEWART.

To Captain F———.

Marine Barracks, Portsmouth,
February 8th, 1811.

I received your letter yesterday, my dear brother, and immediately went to the barracks, to make the necessary inquiries respecting the young man you mentioned, who had enlisted into our corps.

A person of that description, had been at quarters, but is now embarked on board the Conquestador, fifty guns, but I shall go on board and find him out, and use every means to make him sensible of his error.

The Captain commanding the marines on board, is an intimate friend of mine, I shall, therefore, immediately acquaint him with the circumstance. I have not yet received any answer to my application to Sir David Dundas.

Having this moment read the orders, I find, I am on a court-martial to-morrow, in waiting the next day, and on guard the following; but I do not complain, for the duty is trivial, as we shall have some little more relief, when the officers come round from Chatham. Your pictures will be sent off next week, but I will give you notice.

February the 15th. Your letter was put into my hands, while I was sitting on a court-martial, which has kept us employed three days. Upon inquiry, I found the young man was discharged from the ship, and found him at Mr. C——'s, according to your direction. I had some conversation with him, on the subject of his leaving his friends; he informed me, that his uncle did not use him unkindly, he had only a few words with him. He appears a promising youth ;* I invited him to breakfast with me.

And now, my dear brother, to my own business.

* Now, senior Captain, in a native regiment of cavalry, in India, having the command of a subsidiary force of 1,000 native horse—lost his right arm.

I was gazetted this day, in the ninety-fifth regiment, and my resignation is gone up to the Admiralty. I have been nearly seven years in the marines, and stand, as to rank, according to the Royal Navy List, at the head of 486 lieutenants, viz : 146 first lieutenants, and 340 second lieutenants, being nearly the oldest first lieutenant of 1808.

February the 21st. The acceptance of my resignation came down to-day, therefore I shall take leave of Portsmouth, on Saturday morning. I am just in time, as I stood again first for foreign service.

London, February the 27th. I arrived here on Saturday evening, and by the advice of Mr. Adair, I wrote to Colonel Wade, commanding officer at Hythe, stating my wish, to be allowed a month or six weeks leave of absence, to recruit my strength, not being able, at present, to encounter the fatigues of actual service. I have this moment received his answer, informing me that he has forwarded my application to Colonel Torrens, and I am now awaiting the result.

Copy of a letter from Alexander Adair, Esq. agent to the ninety-fifth.

Pall Mall, February 15th, 1811.

SIR,

I have now the pleasure to acquaint you, that a notification has been made out, appointing your brother a second Lieutenant, in the second battalion, ninety-fifth regiment, whose commission, when signed, will bear date 21st November, 1810. Should he not be in Portugal, it may be proper for him to join a detachment of the battalion at Hythe, unless he should receive other orders.

I am, Sir,

Your most obedient servant,

ALEXANDER ADAIR.

To Captain F——.

London, March the 10th, 1811. I have been anticipating, my dear brother, the pleasure of seeing you, and have been endeavouring to accomplish my intentions, without the expense of a journey to Hythe, however, this cannot be done, agreeably to the present regulations of the army, which enjoins all officers to appear first at head-quarters, to report themselves, after appointment, in order that any application for leave, may be forwarded through the general officer commanding the district.

Colonel Wade has written to me, saying, that he has not the least objection to my taking my leave of absence, without first joining, could it be so managed.

I produced his letter to the Adjutant-General, but found the order imperative, therefore I purpose setting out to join my regiment to-morrow.

.Upper Barracks, Hythe, March the 17th, 1811. I should have answered your letter of the 13th, by return of post, but I had not then seen the Colonel.

I am much obliged to you, my dear brother, for the trouble and anxiety you have had in writing to him, respecting my leave. He was so kind as to send off the application by an orderly dragoon, as soon as possible.

I have not made any effort, to effect an exchange to the third battalion, as you do not approve it. The Colonel is very kind, particularly, as I have been again unwell, he was so attentive as to visit my sick room. He remembers you a lieutenant of light infantry, at Weymouth, in 1801.

My brother officers wish me to remain in this battalion, many of them are musical, and we have had already, several amateur concerts.

I met your worthy friend, (Mr. H. H. W.) in town, we dined at Gibson's, and also at Mr. B———'s, and we breakfasted twice together. The evening before I left, I spent the evening at my respected friend's Colonel ———. I hope to be with you on the 1st of April, my leave extending to the 21st of May. I have received the following letters of approbation, from three of my late commanding officers of the royal marines.

Portsmouth, 21st of February, 1811.

DEAR SIR,

I feel much pleasure in complying with your request, in bearing testimony to your gentlemanly character, and good conduct during the time I have had the pleasure of serving with you in the royal marines. I have every reason to believe you to be a good and zealous officer, and I most sincerely hope, by the exchange you have made, (as it will afford you a more distinguished field for your abilities,) that your utmost wishes may be gratified.

I am, dear Sir,

Very truly yours,

J. MILLER,*

Lieutenant-Colonel, R. M.

To Lieutenant F——.

Portsmouth, 22nd of February, 1811.

MY DEAR SIR,

I am extremely sorry I had not the pleasure of shaking you by the hand, prior to your leaving Portsmouth, it would have given me much satisfaction, as your general good conduct, and gentlemanly behaviour, during your service in the corps, has been such as to insure you the good wishes of all your brother officers; should it be in my power at any time to serve you, I hope you will not hesitate a moment to command me, and whenever you return to this, or any other place where I may have a house, I hope you will give me the opportunity of proving how much I am,

My dear Sir,

Your sincere friend, and well-wisher,

JOHN BOSCAWEN SAVAGE,†

Major, R. M.

To Lieutenant F——.

---

* Since dead.   † Colonel Commandant, R.M. at Chatham.

Portsmouth, February 1st, 1811.

I have much satisfaction in bearing testimony to the correct conduct of Lieutenant F——, of the royal marines, while serving under my command, on board H. M. ship Diadem. We served together from the commencement of 1805, at the conquest of the Cape of Good Hope, and the reduction of Buenos Ayres, until the 12th of August, 1806, when we mutually became prisoners. During the whole of each period, I had the strongest cause to respect him as a gentleman, and as a good and zealous officer.

ALEXANDER GILLESPIE.

Captain, R. M.

Lieutenant F—— rejoined the ninety-fifth regiment, after the expiration of his leave of absence.

Ashford Barracks, May the 27th. You will be surprised, my dear brother, at seeing this dated from Ashford, instead of Hythe, but on my arrival at this latter place, I found that Colonel Wade had received an intimation from the Commander-in-chief, that he had been pleased to transfer Lieutenant F—— to the third battalion, ninety-fifth regiment.

The Colonel thinks that General Stewart must have been the occasion of it. The officers of the second battalion expressed their regret, and wished me much to remain, having planned out several musical parties.

The Commanding Officer of the third battalion, Major John, is an excellent manager, and remarkably particular, as to the gentlemanly conduct and appearance of his officers : the battalion is fine, and well appointed. Two officers are going from hence to Cadiz, to fill up the vacancies of two, who have been severely wounded ; also two from Hythe are under similar orders, this is all the news at present. I am sorry to learn, that it is not likely to come to my turn at present, unless the whole of the regiment be ordered abroad, as there are two or three seniors to me.

July the 15th. I do, my dearest brother, most sincerely condole with you, on your severe loss ; the dispensation is an afflicting one, yet you have many comforts remaining. To that merciful Providence I commit you and your dear family, who ever administers consolation when He afflicts.

August the 22nd. We are under some expectation of proceeding soon to Spain. General Nichols has inspected us, and has given a most flattering report of us to the Commander-in-chief; that we are in the highest state of discipline, and the finest description of men he had ever seen. On this inspection I was ordered to take the command of a company from a senior officer, which occasioned some words between us: I told him that I should not allow him to say any more on the subject, and if he found himself aggrieved, he must apply to the commanding officer, as I had only obeyed orders.

I am residing in the same house with the Major and his family, as well as my friend Lieutenant

F——.* We pass our evenings very agreeably. We attended a ball a few days ago, given by Lieutenant-General Harris to the families of this neighbourhood.

The Hon. Major-General Stewart has arrived in England, for the recovery of his wounds, received at the battle of Albuera, when he made that gallant charge and drove the French from the heights. Captain Percival saw him in town, and found him convalescent; he was some time his aid-de-camp. The General inquired after me. I intend writing, to congratulate him on his safe arrival. We keep close at our drill, and have been manœuvring ever since daylight, throwing our advanced guard towards Canterbury.

Upper Hythe Barracks, November the 11th. We received a route for these barracks rather suddenly, to be stationed here till further orders. As there appears little prospect of going on service at present, it is my intention to apply for leave, as soon as an officer joins, to take charge of my company. We skirmish every day upon the cliffs, whenever the weather will permit. We have good society in this neighbourhood; I am going to B—— Park, to a musical party.

December the 10th. We march to-morrow morning for Shorncliff barracks, where we shall remain till we leave England. I rode over to this place the other day, being a few miles distant, and the first

* Now a Lieut.-Col. unattached.

object that presented itself, close under our future barrack, was a ship in a thousand pieces, wrecked on the preceding night : —— Park is near this place, the residence of a delightful family ; and they have given me a general invitation to go whenever my duties will permit.

December the 16th. I am very anxious to get on service, but all my efforts are unavailing, as I am obliged to await my turn. Our new quarter affords us much better accommodation than our former one. The situation is far better adapted for riflemen, owing to the irregular face of the country, and the variety of positions, in a military point of view, suits our new method of drill, and enlarges the knowledge of the duties of riflemen.

We are under the command of General Murray : the second and third battalions of the ninety-fifth are engaged to fire at a target, for a prize given by Lady Murray. I am in hopes we shall win it, as our men practise daily. We tried a new movement the other day, before the General, firing ball at a target, re-treating in four lines, which was much approved. It was the first trial, and appeared hazardous, yet no accident happened. I have received the General's permission to go on leave, and intend being in town, next Wednesday or Thursday.

London, December the 30th. I have been con-fined here a week, by a bad foot, occasioned by my horse treading on it when dismounting : it swelled so much, that it was necessary to cut off my boot ;

however it is now nearly well. G—— called
this morning, and wished me to take a coach, and
go to his father's ; but I declined it.   I have met
with a few Roman coins for you, and they have been
seen by Sir Joseph Banks, who pronounced them
genuine, and wished to purchase them.

December 31st.—I have called this morning upon
my gallant Colonel, the Hon. Major-General Stewart.   He received me in the most friendly manner,
greeting me, " I am happy to see you at last, after
so many disappointments ;" he hoped our acquaint-
ance would improve.   He described to me the different positions of the battle of Albuera, where he
received his wounds : he spoke of his regiment with
great animation, said he had seen it in every trying
situation, and that the riflemen were gallant fellows.
He pressed me to stay with him, but I pleaded my
leaving town to-morrow. He sent his kind respects to
you, that as soon as he heard of anything worth your
acceptance, you should hear from him.

Lieutenant F—— arrived in Staffordshire, on
leave, which was prolonged until the 10th of March,
1812.

Copy of a letter from Major John, ninety-fifth
regiment.

My dear F——,

Upon the receipt of your letter, requesting an
extension of leave to the 10th of March, I lost no

time in making the necessary application to Major-
General Mackenzie, who has been pleased to grant
it, but not in time for me to write by yesterday's
post, as I wished and intended to have done; but
this will reach you, I hope, in time to prevent your
being put to the least inconvenience. F——'s leave
is prolonged to the same period.

I see nothing like an immediate prospect of service, but are in a fair way of having plenty of drill,
under an officer that understands the thing well,
and from whom we are likely to derive much useful
instruction.

I have appointed you and F—— to S——'s company. H—— has joined us, and a new officer of
the name of F——r.

Believe me always to be,

Most faithfully yours,

HENRY JOHN.

To Lieutenant F——,
    3rd battalion, 95th.

Copy of a letter from the Hon. Major-General
Stewart.

London, Oct. 12th, 1811.

MY DEAR SIR,

I am gratified to learn your brother's partiality to his present corps; he is, I doubt not, a
valuable acquisition. I wish that obstacles had not
so long prevented his entry to it; he is, however,

advancing by tolerably good strides towards his company.

I have the honour to be, my dear Sir,

Your very faithful humble servant,

WILLIAM STEWART.

To Captain F——.

Shorncliff, March 13th, 1812.—I should have written to you yesterday, my dear brother, but I was so much indisposed that I was really obliged to defer it. I met my friend F—— in town on the Sunday, and we agreed to set out the following morning from the Borough ; but eventually took the Dover mail, and posted from thence to this place, where we arrived about four o'clock on Tuesday.

We have, as yet, received no intimation of service, though the wing is in perfect readiness to march at an hour's notice. I am first for duty, and by the death of Captain Uniack of our battalion, after poor Hawkesley's, who fell at the storming of Ciudad Rodrigo, a vacancy has occurred in the right wing, but will not be officially known till the next returns arrive from the Peninsula ; I hope then to be allowed to go out. I trust we shall meet again, my dear brother, ere long.—Farewell!

It is singular, but not less true, a short time before poor Hawkesley went out, we used to joke him upon the privations he would suffer on actual service, as he had never been abroad. When the order arrived for his departure, he was much depressed, saying he could not account for it, but he felt a presentiment that he never should return.   He never did return —he fell in the breach, in advancing to the storming of Ciudad Rodrigo, and had a soldier's grave; not in consecrated ground, but where he fell, in the breach of the fortress.

April 10th.—The only wish I have at this moment is, to be in Portugal before the fall of Badajos; but I fear I shall not, although the Major tells me to expect an order very soon ; but I distrust the word *soon*, I have been too much accustomed to it.

We are now in prime order, and are much commended by the General commanding here.   Your sentiments respecting our gallant regiment, are, I believe, not misapplied, and feel the compliment flattering, as coming from an old soldier.   As to the general duties of our profession, I accord with you, that a life of danger is far preferable to living amongst the illiberal; however, my dear brother, as you are situated, it would not be prudent for you to give way to such feelings, although perfectly consonant with the profession of arms.   Your life is valuable to those who have so many claims upon it, and this should supersede all other considerations.

Are not these your own sentiments, my dear brother?   Indeed, so far am I convinced that you do not value life on your own account, that were I to be called into the field this moment, I should wish no better example than yours, as a guide to enable me to discharge my duties, and to meet with fortitude the fate of a soldier.

If an order do not arrive soon for our embarkation, we expect to be sent to some quarter to receive volunteers from the militia, which will occupy us for three weeks or more.

April 26th.—My last letter to you arrived, I understand, on the very evening of your departure, consequently, you did not get it until your return. The official accounts of the fall of Badajos, by storm, have arrived, and a most sanguinary conflict it has been.   A private letter was received here yesterday from the scene of action, with the latest accounts of our brother officers who have fallen.

In the first place, seven are killed belonging to our battalion, besides wounded ; —some of them only left us a month ago.   In the course of an hour or two, there were twenty-four rifle officers killed and wounded.   The fifty-second regiment has suffered severely, having lost sixteen or eighteen officers.   This regiment and the ninety-fifth, principally led the storming party on the first onset ; however, the points attacked were so strong, and the slaughter so dreadful, (for the men faced death with the utmost fortitude,) that the Commander-in-chief had them recalled, and directed an attack on a more assailable quarter, which was followed up with success.

This regimental havoc will give me my promotion : the General commanding here, thinks it very likely that the whole of the left wing will be ordered out to relieve the right.   The assembly has sounded, and it is my turn to manœuvre the battalion to-day, according to orders.

Another letter has arrived, dated Badajos, with some particulars of our wounded officers.   Lieutenant Macdonald died soon after the despatches were closed ; and as soon as his death is notified to the war-office, I expect to be gazetted as a first lieutenant.   The officer in his letter, says, that such a scene of carnage was never before witnessed by the oldest soldier there.

On the first onset, the light division had upwards of seventy officers, and 996 rank and file, killed and wounded.   Seven officers of the ninety-fifth regiment fell at the same moment, in mounting the breach, which was mined and countermined with double rows of shells, and other combustibles.   The avenues leading to every street were deeply entrenched, and lined with cannon, charged with grape-shot, &c.   Many of our wounded officers are not likely to recover.

May 7th.—I should have noticed your letter of the 26th ult. sooner, but I did not receive it until my return from Dover, where I had been to receive volunteers from the English militia.

As the happiness of yourself, my dear brother, as well as that of the dear friends around you, has ever been one of my first wishes, it is almost unnecessary

to tell you, that any event which may tend to promote it, will always give me the most sincere and
heartfelt pleasure.

With respect to myself, my opinion remains un-
changed, and when I think otherwise, it is more than
probable I shall cease to exist; however, the fortune
of war may decide that point, much sooner than my
calculation, and put my unchangeable thoughts out
of countenance. Well! come when it will, I think
I shall never flinch, and at all events, shall not be
taken by surprise.

The occurrences of this life are certainly *very, very*
changeable and uncertain; for instance—a rifleman
of ours was married the other day, and the regimental band played the new couple to and from church.
The day following, we went out to fire ball at the
target, when this same rifleman was shot through the
breast by accident, and died immediately on the
ground : strange to tell, the band that played before
him to church when married, now played the Dead
March in Saul, to the same place, for him to be
buried, within the short space of fifty-eight hours.

How chequered is human life ! The man bore an
excellent character : we much regretted the fatal
accident.

I am pushing all the interest I can make, to go
out to Portugal before I am gazetted to a first lieutenancy. Three of us are under orders. Is General
B———, now serving in the Peninsula, the friend of
Colonel M———?

May 15th.—My brother having been absent from home some time, I address you, my dear Miss A——, to thank you for your very welcome and kind letter. I received it with much satisfaction and pleasure.

I could say much in reply to it, but my spirits are sadly depressed at this time, therefore you will excuse my brevity. To account for this somewhat singular style of writing, I have to relate a sad event, very painful to my feelings, which took place on Wednesday last, and has made me very miserable; to relieve my mind there is no alternative, but to inform you; to be brief then,—by an accident, as fatal as unforeseen,—I have taken away the life of a fellow-soldier!

Our regiment was at exercise, firing ball at the target. I took a loaded rifle from one of the men, to try the range, and with the intention of explaining to the men also the new mode of firing recommended to riflemen, the piece went off in my hand, by accident, while holding it by my side, and instead of its killing me, which might have been the case, the ball passed through the body of a fine young man, who was placed to mark the target, about the distance of 150 yards from me. I heard him cry out, and saw him fall instantly, never to rise again in this world!

Words cannot express my unutterable anguish on reaching the spot,—forgive me when I say, I envied the poor dying soldier's situation at the moment. O! indeed, could it have saved the life of the unfortunate victim, freely would I have given my own. A short time before this melancholy catastrophe, I was rejoicing at the near prospect of joining the British army in Spain—I am now inconsolable! How very defective is our foresight, in this world of trouble and sorrow! How has my ambition been laid prostrate!

I have not left my room since the unhappy event, nor can I muster resolution to do so, except to proceed to the place of embarkation; write to me again soon. The kindness of my brother officers has been marked towards me, particularly that of my commanding officer, who has been sitting with me to-day, talking over this unfortunate occurrence. The General's opinion is, that no blame whatever attaches to me on the charge of inattention, and that such an accident would have happened to himself, had he, in the same instance, taken up the rifle, which, upon inspection, has been declared defective. All this may be consolatory in one point of view, but it does not relieve the acuteness of my feelings; of which no one, unless in a similar situation, can form a just estimate.

The first fatal accident, (which I have so recently noticed,) drew forth an observation from me, " That I should not like to encounter the feelings of the unfortunate man who was the cause of it;" little dreaming that a similar event hung over my head.

An application has been forwarded to the war-office, for the Commander-in-chief's permission to allow me to join the army abroad with Lord Wellington. I am anxiously awaiting it : my friend F—— goes with me.

London, May 23rd. — I wished much to have written to you, my dear brother, before this, but your long absence from home deprived me of this gratification. I have had much on my mind lately, the cause of which you are of course, by this time, fully acquainted with, I shall therefore be spared the painful task of recapitulation.

I experienced much relief from the letter I received from the kind and affectionate friend of your children, Miss A——, and hope that a change of scene, which I am now likely to encounter on active service, the bustle of a campaign, and the daily view of the enemy, will divert the present current of my thoughts into another channel.

I could say much to you, my dearest brother, on this subject, but time presses, having just arrived in town, on my way to Portsmouth, to embark for Lisbon. Your very kind and friendly letter is this moment put into my hand. Part of our regiment marched from Shorncliff, yesterday morning, to the place of embarkation. I shall join them on their march thither, on Wednesday night or the following morning. I have several commissions for my brother officers, who are with the detachment, and shall join them time enough to march into Portsmouth, where we embark forthwith for the seat of war.

I am now a first lieutenant, and have received orders to act as such, although not yet gazetted, being the senior second lieutenant of the three battalions. I have purchased saddle, bridle, spy-glass, portable soup, &c. With regard to an application of being allowed to take rank as a first lieutenant, you will have the goodness to consult with the Major.

May 27th.—I am happy to inform you, my dear brother, that my spirits are improving; the immediate prospect of active service revives all the energies of the soldier, and the duties of the field stand paramount. I am leaving town to-night by the mail.—Farewell!

CHAPTER XI.

Embarkation for the Peninsula, until his arrival in England, in May 1813, *after the retreat of the army from Burgos.*

CORA, Transport, No. 241, Spithead, June 6th, 1812.—I received your letter, my dear brother, with its enclosure, for which accept my best thanks.

I must request of you to receive the remainder of the prize money, for the capture of Buenos Ayres, which will be paid in the course of this month. The amount, I am glad to say, will be eighty or one hundred pounds, but it is said will amount to £120.; but I shall be satisfied if I get either of the above sums. The reason of this unexpected payment is, the Leda frigate has been thrown out of sharing in the capture.

With respect to my baggage, my dearest brother, I shall not trouble you, except—I fall; you will then write to the head quarters of the ninety-fifth, in England, every thing will be found in the regimental stores, and of course will be delivered over to you.

I should not wish anything sold : my pictures, and silver-mounted Mamlouk sabre, (the one worn by you in the West Indies, and which I value,) I have left in charge of my kind friend, the Major, at Shorncliff, who has undertaken the care of them until my return; but if that period should never arrive, you will receive the sword with the other things. I have presented the Major with one or two pictures ; but those I brought home with me the last time, you will receive safe, viz. Andreas Hofer, a landscape, and one of our late dear brother William's. I recollect my dearest mother expressed a wish for that of Andreas Hofer, therefore, if I should never return, my wish is, to have it given to my beloved and estimable parent, as the last tribute from her affectionate and dutiful son.

As to money matters, I shall leave every thing with you, my dear brother, to settle for me, feeling assured that whatever arrangements you may make, they will be just and proper. After settling these trifling affairs, my spirits are improving, all things considered; and if ever I should be thrown into a situation where my humble exertions may be required, I hope, my dear brother, neither you, or any of my dear friends, will ever have any cause to blush for me.

I have an excellent tempered sword, made on purpose for me, by Reddle of Piccadilly, who has made for many general officers. The wind is becoming fair, and we expect to sail this day. I have a letter

of introduction from Lady —— ——, to her brother, Lieutenant-Colonel ——, which I have left
with my friend G——, who will await your deter-
mination thereupon.

I shall leave it to you to address the Hon. Major-
General Stewart, respecting my claims for back rank,
and the Major will write to you upon the subject.
Since I have been here, the kindness of my Portsmouth friends has been marked indeed. You do
not know, my dear brother, what comfort I derived
from your very kind letter. I was much pleased to
receive a letter from my dear sister; I will write to
my dearest father and mother very soon; kiss your
dear children for me,—farewell! Two very fine
young men have joined us here, to go out as volunteers.

Cora transport, at sea, June 7th. I take advantage of the pilot's leaving the ship, to send you a
few lines more, before we take our final departure
from the English shores. The wind is come round
suddenly, which prevents my writing a long letter;
however, it will be satisfactory, and not the less acceptable. I fortunately met the Commodore late
last evening, who informed me that he should sail at
daylight; of course I went on board immediately,
although it was midnight, and in my haste have left
many things behind, which I shall want in Spain.

I was happy in receiving a letter from my dear
sister, informing me of the good health of my dear
father and mother, the former going a journey: God

bless them both. We are clearing the land once more, farewell. I shall write from Lisbon.

———

Copy of a letter from John Gibson, Esq.

Admiralty, June 2nd, 1812.

MY DEAR SIR,

I have the honour of your letter of the 31st of May, and shall with great pleasure, strictly attend to its contents. I am in great hopes that your letter will have reached your brother this morning, for even supposing the transports ready, (which I very much doubt, as no application has been made for convoying them out to Portugal,) the wind will prevent their sailing, it is now S.W., and has been ever since he left London. Your brother was very cheerful when in town, and looked forward to his campaign with great hope.

His service in Spain or Portugal will be arduous, and very trying to the constitution in general, but Robert has been so well seasoned to different climates, and used to the toils of an active military life, that he will not feel the inconvenience so much as a young inexperienced officer. His talents and activity, I am very confident, will soon raise him to that rank in the army, which he so eminently deserves.

June the 8th. Enclosed is a letter from your brother ; he sailed yesterday, in the Cora transport, and has of course received your letter. I shall be most happy to forward your letters to him, as usual.

June the 26th. I have delayed answering your letter of the 11th instant, that I might have an opportunity of consulting Captain Kempster, respecting the prize money due to your brother, but his return from Portsmouth is uncertain, therefore shall wait no longer. I understand that no person can receive pay or prize money belonging to any officer, without a regular power of attorney. The letter in your possession may probably answer the purpose, therefore, if you will have the goodness to send it to me, at your earliest opportunity, I will go to the office where the money will be paid, and make the necessary inquiries.

The agent of the ninety-fifth, of course, has a power of attorney, but I should wish you to receive the money without its passing through the hands of any agent whatever, as they charge commission and agency, upon all sums which they either pay or receive.

> Believe me, dear Sir,
>> Yours most faithfully,
>>> JOHN GIBSON.

To Captain F———.

Copy of a letter from Major John, respecting Lieutenant F——'s claim for back rank.

Shorncliff Barracks, 17th of June, 1812.

Sir,

I have had the honour of receiving your letter of the 11th instant, and although every way disposed and desirous to serve your brother, and to promote his interest in getting forward in his profession, yet I am free to confess, I feel at a loss what to advise in the present instance, which is a novel case. That your brother is a first lieutenant ere this, there can scarcely be a doubt, vice Macdonald shot through the lungs, therefore having succeeded to that step, would not his former services in the marines, come in better by and by, in his memorial, upon a favourable opportunity, for a company?

I am not clear that he would be allowed to take rank in the line from the date of his former commission, the two services being distinct; but admitting that he applied, and obtained the back rank in the army, (for it would not be given him in the ninety-fifth,) what would he gain by it?—certainly no rank in his present regiment, and if in this instance, his request was complied with, it might be considered a great favour, and that he would have no further claims; whereas, if he reserve the mention of his services, for a future memorial, they may help him to a company; and advancement of that sort from the seat of war, would be certainly attended to.

Thus, Sir, I have candidly stated to you my senti-

P

ments ; but let me request you, not to be influenced by any thing I have said, lest it might affect your brother's future walk in life.

I would advise you to consult abler judges than I am, upon so important a point.   Of my support and assistance, my friend F——— may always depend, and with that assurance, I have the honour to be,

Very much yours,

HENRY JOHN.

To Captain F———.

Lieutenant F——— was promoted in the gazette of June the 16th, 1812 ; viz. second Lieutenant Robert F——— to be first Lieutenant, vice Macpherson dead.—Commission date 11th of June.

Lisbon, June the 26th, Convent de la Carma. You have, my dear brother, ere this received my last letter from Portsmouth, acknowledging the receipt of yours, and its enclosure ; it was written in great haste, and scarcely intelligible, as may be the case with my future letters, while on actual service, but hope they will not be less acceptable to a brother soldier, who is well acquainted with the accustomed privations, incidental to our professional career.

These inconveniences already alluded to, are practically felt, as I am writing to you from the cell of a monk, belonging to the convent, and which cell I purpose making my bedchamber to-night, upon some good clean straw.

One of the monks has lent me a small table, at which I am now writing, with a bottle of wine, a candle stuck in the neck of it, by way of candlestick, and the candle in its turn, serving as a cork to the bottle, to prevent the wine getting flat.

The whole of our men, two companies of riflemen, (about 200) are quartered in the convent; the monks having given up so many cells to us, and are in every respect remarkably civil : we march the day after to-morrow, to join Lord Wellington. The light division to which we belong, is about 600 miles up the country, and is still on the advance, rendering it uncertain when we shall join them.

The French are on the move, to attack General Hill, and we are anxious to be up in time. Our march will occupy us a month or six weeks, as the country is mountainous. We are providing ourselves with horses and mules, to carry us, our baggage, and provisions, as some part of the country is destitute. Each officer has orders to provide himself with a horse to ride, and a mule to carry his luggage.

The price of mules is so high, that it is scarcely possible to get one for less than 90 or 100 dollars, and a very prime one, is worth from 130 to 140. Every rifle officer is allowed forage for one of each while on service, and this allowance is double to that of officers of other regiments. I feel at a loss for hard dollars, and unless I can get a bill cashed, must go without a horse, which is so essential for our long march; therefore I shall draw upon you for £20 or £30.

The army is two or three months in arrears of pay, on account of the scarcity of dollars, which obliges each one to live upon his daily rations, up the country; so money is not much wanted after leaving Lisbon ; however, it is as well to be provided with a little, for much comfort has been experienced in having it, particularly in the event of being wounded ; however, if I cannot get my bill negotiated, I must submit, and march, like many other soldiers, with an empty pocket. Well, I shall have the less care about me, and others to keep me in countenance.

The weather is so intensely hot, that we shall proceed on our route during the night, and rest in the day-time. We had a tolerable passage from England, but, as usual, I suffered much from sea-sickness, and for three or four days was very ill. Your very kind letter, my dearest brother, did much to restore my spirits.

Several of our officers are at Lisbon, for the recovery of their wounds. It is really wonderful to hear of the hair-breadth escapes some of them had at Badajos. Lieutenant M——, on whom I called this morning, is very severely wounded, and going to England, with a year's leave of absence ; a grape-shot hit him, mounting the breach, he fell into the ditch, and lay there covered with the dead and the dying, until all was over, unable to help himself, having been trampled upon by the light division on their advance to the assault.

Another who had mounted the walls, took hold of the chevaux de frieze, it gave way, and he fell headlong into the ditch. It is now bed-time—good night: I believe that I am the only person up in the convent. The monk who has been sitting with me, has been relating the outrages of the French when at Lisbon, and pointing out the different places where they entered, observing, that had it not been for the English, they would all have been put to death. I have promised to breakfast with him, if I can, to-morrow morning. The convent is still, and looks very dismal, with a few faint lights hanging in the different archways, and the bells tolling at intervals.

June the 27th. Good morning, my dear brother; I have this moment left my straw, and feel much refreshed after a sound sleep : if I never meet with a worse bed during the time I shall be in Portugal, I shall have very little cause of complaint. How delighted I shall be to hear from you when up the country.

Ciudad Rodrigo, July the 19th. I intended to have written to my dearest parents by this convey-ance, but must defer it until my arrival at Sala-manca, as my frank contains already, letters to the Major and Eeles on money matters, to arrange, if possible, a plan to get cash advanced to me if I should want it.

Some of the officers here have been nine months

without pay, and in cases of wounds, or being made prisoner, great privations have been experienced. Indeed repeated instances of this nature have occurred ; there are officers lying here, with whom I have been conversing, who are miserable examples of this. I have, therefore, written to the Major to request Eeles, paymaster of the left wing at home, to write to his brother paymaster of the right wing, to which our detachment belongs, as soon as possible, that is, when he has received an order from you, to authorise me to draw on him in advance.

You will please, therefore, to remit to the Major £30 or £35 to be given to the paymaster, and he will direct me to draw on the paymaster with the army, if necessary; stating at the same time, that he has effects of mine in his hands at home, to that amount. I know of no other plan, as there is scarcely any public money with the army, and the issue of pay very uncertain.

It is reported that an attack was made upon the military chest at Salamanca by banditti, who attempted to force the guard during the night, after our troops had moved forward. I find myself getting too small for my wearing apparel, in consequence of hard work and little to eat. I have lived upon chocolate for several days, and in case of a wound, I shall stand a better chance in not being too well fed.

We have just been informed, that Lord Wellington is preparing for some important blow, and the

army look forward to him with confidence; for we
have received directions this morning to proceed as
quick as possible; as our services are required, and
orders are given to march. We hope to reach the
army in seven days; the scene of action is twelve
or fourteen leagues beyond Salamanca.

My legs and feet swelled so much a few days ago,
that I felt alarmed, but am glad to say I am now
able to continue the march. My friend F——— is
not able to proceed with us, and it is with the deep-
est regret I add, that he must be left at a vile little
town on the frontiers of Portugal. I fear the campaign will be too much for him. I am very anxious
about him, but the same thing would have happened
to me had I continued ill.

The interior of Portugal is bold and magnificent,
the prospect from the mountains is not to be described, but the towns and inhabitants are wretched
indeed. Happy England! what a contrast! Since
we have entered Spain we have observed a considerable difference, both in the towns and the people,
particularly in their conduct towards us; they seem
more happy to see us than the Portuguese.

The weather is intensely hot, and the marches
very trying; we have generally moved at midnight,
but the heat then, is almost insupportable. Many
of our men are left ill upon the road. The fatigue
of marching in this country is great; but do not
suppose I complain, O no, it is only the beginning,
our share is not yet dealt out. I have not had my

clothes off now, nearly a month, but this is a trifle to a soldier, as times go here.

I am still annoyed by violent pains in my head, but attribute it to the overpowering heat. I carry a blanket under my horse's saddle, and spread it on the ground when we halt, for my bed. If we remain a few hours in Salamanca I will write again, but I hope we shall soon come into action.

In marching thus at midnight, my thoughts often wander towards home, and I almost fancy myself in Staffordshire, when the stumbling of my horse rouses me from my agreeable reveries. I must now inquire after your dear family, and their kind and affectionate friend, though last mentioned, not the least thought of, or less admired for her excellent qualities.

I have just been to visit the grave of a brother officer, poor Hawkesley; and the place where he was shot. His military career was short, but glorious ; his grave, the bed of honour. I could not help turning over in my mind, how short a time since we were leaning on each side of my chimney-piece at Shorncliff, seriously talking over the dangers of active service. I walked away from H——'s grave in sadness, lamenting his untimely fate. Ciudad Rodrigo appears to have been much battered, like many of the towns we have passed through, made examples, (as the French term it,) for their attachment to their legal government ; the enemy mark their line of retreat by devastation and cruelty.

I have annexed our route from Lisbon to Sala-

manca; from the latter place we take a fresh one.
Let me hear from you very soon ; pray send me all
particulars of my dear friends.   Twenty-four waggons full of sick are arrived from the army, as this
place is to be head quarters ; the following is the
route of the two companies of riflemen.   Some of the
places named are not laid down in the map, at all
events, you can follow our line of march to Salamanca ; I do not know the names of the places in our
new march.

Sacavem	St. Miguel
Villa Franca	Menissa
Azambuja	Sabujàl
Santarem	Nava
Golegam	Aldea de Ponte
Punhete	Altejaro
Abrantes	Huero
Gaviao	Ciudad Rodrigo
Niza	Santo Espíritus
Villa Velha	Castilijue de Phana
Panados	Castio
Castel Branco	Salamanca
Eschalos de Cuima	

July the 22nd : Near Salamanca.   All my arrangements are upset, I intended to have sent you a
very long letter, but the enemy will prevent it.

After marching through Portugal and part of Spain
in search of the British army, without any correct
tidings of them, we have at last got into the thick

of it.   The light division, to which we belong, is at
this moment engaged with the French ; we can hear
their music, which though not very soft, is reviving
to the ear of a soldier, who has been toiling days and
nights in search of it; we have now our object in
view, and hope soon to get up to add to its animat-
ing sounds ;—when our men are refreshed we shall
proceed.

We are but a few miles from Salamanca, but fear
we shall not see it, although Lord Wellington was
there last night, but reports are not to be relied
upon.

Our troops are now in order of battle, and the
enemy inclined for a general action.   At this moment they are at it ; we are pushing forward, and
expect to be up in time.   The roads are already
covered with the sick and wounded; the inhabitants
of Salamanca, and of the surrounding villages are
flying in various directions; the confusion is general.
We are again urged forward by an order just received, so that I am obliged to leave my day's allowance of food behind, which is a little chocolate on
the fire.

Salamanca, July 23rd.—We are this moment arrived, after marching during the night, but late in the
action.   The French have suffered severely ; 3,000
prisoners are just made near us.   The field presents
a sad sight, an awful lesson of mortality.   The sabre cuts, inflicted by our cavalry upon the wounded,

are frightful, some of their faces being nearly oblite-
rated, others with dangerous cuts upon the head,
arms, and legs.

I was shocked to observe the Spaniards, robbing
those who were in the agonies of death ; one unfortunate sufferer was stripped of every thing, although
he had received three balls, besides sabre wounds,
and part of a bayonet remained in his body; in this
state he lay exposed, though not dead. I came up
while they were in the act of robbing another
Frenchman, who begged my assistance ; I put a
stop to the cruelty of the plunderers. The man
seemed thankful, and asked me for a bit of bread,
which I gave him, soaked in wine ; but he, like the
other poor fellow, was so dreadfully mangled by the
sabre, that he could not swallow it. I never saw
such severe wounds in the course of my service.

The French are in full retreat, and we are in pursuit of them, forming the advanced guard. My letter is incoherent, but I snatch the time as it flies.
We are about fording the river above Salamanca, intending early in the morning to pursue the retreating
army on the road to Madrid. The French are still
retiring in great confusion, leaving their sick and
wounded behind ; their cavalry so knocked up and
disabled, that they are falling into our hands every
league.

I have nothing with me but what is on my back,
for all our baggage was ordered back to Ciudad
Rodrigo, where it will remain until our return. Our

troops behaved gallantly, although the French artillery (which was numerous and well served) made great havoc, being twelve pounders, and ranging to a great distance. I regret that we were not up at the commencement of the battle, but our commanding officer did his best. The enemy still in our front, and we in full pursuit. I am prevented sending this letter until another halt, but will enclose it to my friends at Lichfield. We are ordered off.

July 24th.—We are following the enemy on the Madrid road. The field of battle, even now, presents a distressing scene ; the wounded were left on the plain near Salamanca, when we advanced, their wounds not having been attended to ; there was no help for it, the medical assistance was general. The cavalry are now engaged, and we are ordered to advance immediately to support them.

July 25th, Flores del Villa.—After a fatiguing march we again halted, and I have snatched a few moments to resume my pen. The French are on the heights, in our front. I feel much harassed, being kept so much on the alert ; we are now refreshing our men, who are nearly exhausted. At midnight we resume our pursuit, or at daybreak. We hang close upon the enemy's rear, and hope to get hold of them, unless they halt, and give us battle.

Lord Wellington is with us, accompanying the light division himself ; his activity and exertions are astonishing, fatigue is out of the question ; who can complain? It is said that his lordship's skill, in forming his army at the battle of Salamanca, constitutes him the first General of the age.

We have little to eat, and plenty of work ; we are again preparing to advance, the enemy having made a move. You will scarcely be able to make out this scrawl ; I am now writing in the midst of the advanced guard, from my saddle. Do not forget my remittance, I shall want it: where I shall write from next I know not. The advance has just sounded. God bless you all!

Here closes my dear brother's journal, and no tidings were heard of him for some months.

The following letters were received from Major John, of the ninety-fifth regiment, who, as well as myself, was anxious to hear of his welfare.

Shorncliff Barracks,
Sept. 28, 1812.

DEAR SIR,

I have many apologies to make to you for my apparent neglect in not earlier acknowledging the receipt of your letter, covering a draft for £30, for my friend, your brother's use. I shall, however, stand acquitted, I am convinced, in your opinion, of any intentional omission, when I inform you that for these ten weeks past I have been on leave of absence, and that I did not return here until the 24th, when your letter, with many others, was put into my

hand.   I immediately gave orders to Mr. Eeles, our
acting paymaster, who had, previously to my arrival,
given directions to the paymaster on service to give
the credit required to your brother, from whom I
have had the pleasure of receiving one letter since
his arrival in the Peninsula ; he was then well, and
on his way to join the main army.

To hear of his health and welfare, will always be
most gratifying to me, and to promote his wishes, if
ever I have the power, I shall be at all times ready
and willing.   In the event of my hearing anything
particular from Portugal, wherein your brother may
be concerned, I shall not omit to drop you a line; and
if you wish at any time to make inquiries from me
upon the subject, pray do so without scruple, and in
the interim, believe me to be, dear Sir,

Your very obedient
and very humble servant,
HENRY JOHN.

To Captain F——.

Shorncliff, February 10th, 1813.

DEAR SIR,

I have this day received a letter from Colonel
Barnard,* commanding the third battalion, ninety-
fifth, dated 12th of January, wherein he says, that
my friend, your brother, had been extremely ill, but
was recovering fast.   I have reason ere long to ex-

* Major-General Sir A. F. Barnard, K. C. B. and K. C. H.
colonel first battalion, rifle brigade.

pect his arrival in England, for the perfect recovery
of his health; the hardships he went through were
extreme, and you will permit me, with great sincerity,
to rejoice and congratulate you upon his having sur-
mounted them.

Well knowing how gratifying it would be to you
to hear anything satisfactory and certain respecting
your brother, I could not refrain from taking the
liberty of imparting by the earliest post what I had
learnt respecting him.

Upon F———'s return to this country, rely upon
my readiness to meet his wishes in every way within
my power.

I remain, dear Sir,

Your very obedient servant,

HENRY JOHN.

To Captain F———.

Shorncliff Barracks,
Feb. 19, 1813.

DEAR SIR,

In answer to your questions, I beg leave to
inform you that your brother, at the time Colonel
Barnard wrote, was at the head quarters of the light
division, where I presume he now is, for I have this
day received another letter from Colonel Barnard,
dated Galegas, February 2nd, wherein he says,
" T—— and F—— both continue in a weak state,
but I hope they will gain sufficient strength to move

homewards, when the weather becomes milder." So that I hope ere long you may see your brother in this country.

I beg you will never think it necessary to apologise for writing to me, I shall be at all times happy to receive your communications, and in return to give you every information in my power about my friend, respecting whom it is always pleasant to me to write, for I have a very sincere regard for him.

Any information that reaches me, that may be likely to prove acceptable to you, I shall not fail to transmit to you, and in the interim, with best compliments to your family,

I remain, dear Sir,
Very truly your's,
HENRY JOHN.

To Captain F——.

Copy of a letter from John Gibson, Esq.

Admiralty, April 12th, 1813.

MY DEAR SIR,

It is with the greatest satisfaction that I enclose you a letter, received two days ago, (with a power of attorney,) from Robert, whom I had given up for lost. It will be unnecessary to make any comments, it speaks for itself, for I am sure such complicated misfortunes are rarely met with; but, however, the winding up of all is rather pleasant than otherwise, and hope that a short stay in England will make him a better man than ever.

I am, dear Sir,

Your's very sincerely,

JOHN GIBSON.

To Captain F———.

Espeja, near Rodrigo, Spain,
March 4th, 1813.

MY DEAR BROTHER,

I forwarded a power of attorney for you, to my friend Gibson, the duplicate I have forwarded also. I should have written long before this, but severe indisposition prevented me; indeed, I gave up the idea of ever writing more; even now my head will scarcely allow me, it is in such a bewildered state, from extreme debility and suffering. I received, my dear brother, the bill for £30, from the paymaster, but it came a little too late. It was given to me in Salamanca, when very ill, a day or two before the retreat commenced in November, when I lament to say it was lost, with all my other things, or stolen by the attendant during the miserable confusion.

The pleasure of being again able to address my dearest friends, is more than I expected to enjoy again in this world; I assure you, my dearest brother, I have suffered much since I arrived in this country, having been ill upwards of seven months of a violent fever and ague, arising from great exertion and fatigue, in pursuing the enemy after the battle

Q

of Salamanca, which seized me when near Madrid, and what I have suffered since is more than I can describe. [1]

I am now recovering fast, and am recommended by the medical department to proceed to England, as soon as I am able to travel. A medical board was held upon me and another officer of the regiment, and every thing is arranged for our departure, which will take place in a few days; so you may expect to see me in England, please God, in the course of a month or two. I am excessively weak and debilitated, and still subject to ague.

The officer coming home with me is Captain T——, who has been a sufferer with myself. We have a discretionary route to travel as we please, intending to take our journey through Portugal, by easy stages, not more than a league or two each day.

I wrote to my friend Gibson, enclosing one of the powers of attorney, and begged of him to write to you, to say that he had heard from me, or otherwise to forward my letter, thinking it would be more satisfactory until I wrote myself, for I wished to send you an account of my brilliant campaign.

I was taken ill in the beginning of August last, but continued with my regiment for some days, in the hope of getting better, until we arrived near Madrid. I was then very ill, and had become so weak, that I frequently fainted when endeavouring to mount my horse. The surgeon at last ordered me into the rear, and with much difficulty I reached Salamanca in a cart, almost breathing my last; here I lay and grew worse, till I was reduced to a mere skeleton, and had been given over more than once, when our army arrived, with the French at their heels, in November, and every preparation was made to evacuate Salamanca, and to remove the sick further to the rear. Unfortunately, I was too ill to be removed, and the surgeon who attended me, recommended me by all means to make up my mind to be taken prisoner, for he observed, (very humanely, I thought,) that I had no other alternative left, than to be taken by the enemy, or run the risk of losing my life by being removed; for he added without ceremony, that I should surely die before they got me over the bridge, on the outside of the town. I might have died inside the town for him, for I saw him no more; the cannonading had already commenced, the French cavalry had forded the river, and got round our flanks, and I, the only officer in the place, was left to get away how I could.

I now thought it was time to make up my mind to the miserable alternative which my friend, the surgeon, had proposed, for the place was given up to plunder: I was lying unable to stir, in the most dreadful state of suspense, expecting every moment to see a Frenchman pounce in upon me, when to my great astonishment, an officer of my own regiment, (Lieutenant Vickers,) who had heard of my being so shamefully deserted by the hospital surgeon, rushed into the room, determined to rescue me.

He hurried me away, wrapped in a blanket, upon the back of a rifleman, got me put on a cart, and conveyed over the bridge. However, I did not die, as my friend had prognosticated; but if I could have foreseen the misery I afterwards suffered, I should have sooner wished his words had been made good.

We travelled the whole of that night, our army in full retreat, and the French in close pursuit; the weather miserably wet and cold, and the roads so drenched, that it was up to the middle in mud; the animals were knocked up, and I unfortunately fell into the hands of the enemy, a French hussar regiment, who treated me vilely.

They knocked the cart from under me, sabred the men, and dragged me into the middle of the road; stripped me, tearing my clothes into shreds, and turning me over with their sabres, plundered me of what little I had remaining, tore a gold ring from my finger, and then left me naked, to perish with cold and hunger.

I lay in this miserable state two days and nights, with no mortals near me, except dead ones; one of which lay with his head upon my legs, having died in that position during the night preceding, and I was too weak to remove his body; I could not raise myself, I was so reduced.

In this suffering state I continued to exist, which I attribute to some rum, of which I drank a considerable quantity from a Frenchman's canteen, who was humane enough to let me do so, when I ex-

plained to him that I was a British officer. The rum
soon laid me to sleep. The Frenchman was a
hussar, and appeared to belong to the regiment who
had treated me so vilely in the morning, (this happened about dusk.) I begged of him to take me
up behind him; he shook his head, but humanely
took an old blanket from under his saddle, covered
me with it, and then rode off.

The whole of the next day I saw no living soul,
still lying on the road, half famished. The day following an escort of French dragoons came up, with
a number of prisoners, both English and Portuguese,
among them was a soldier of the ninety-fifth, belonging to the same company as myself; he recognised
me, and begged of the Frenchmen to allow him and
three others to remove me to a village, about a
league and a half distant from where I lay.

After some entreaty they consented, as the rifleman declared that he would not leave his officer,
notwithstanding the threats of the French soldiers,
who menaced him with their sabres; but he persisted, saying, that he would sooner die than leave me
to perish.

I was conveyed on their shoulders in a blanket,
almost in a state of insensibility, except when roused
by the inhumanity of the three soldiers, who several
times tumbled me into the mud, in the most unfeeling manner, swearing I was dead, and that they
would carry me no farther; but my rifle comrade
threatened them if they dared to leave me.

During these altercations, I was roused from my stupor, and opening my eyes, assured them that life had not yet ebbed. They carried me to a village which had been plundered, and deserted by the inhabitants. Starvation still stared me in the face, for the escort having laid me inside a hut, proceeded with their prisoners to Salamanca, where I begged in vain they would take me, to save my life, which was then hardly worth preservation; but the idea of being famished to death was dreadful enough, and I could very easily, at that time, have reconciled myself to any other mode of quitting the world.

However, it appears I was to overcome all my disasters. I felt a strong presentiment that I should emerge from this state of suffering, although these men refused to allow any of their prisoners to stay with me, or even to carry me farther, as I was a mere skeleton; they left me in this deserted village, destitute of food and covering.

I still survived, but suffered more from hunger than I can describe, having nothing to subsist upon but horseflesh and acorns, (and both sparingly,) for three weeks or a month, in the depth of winter, part of November and December; during which time, I lay in an old half-unroofed barn, where the Spaniards carried me on their return to the village, without giving me a morsel of bread or food of any sort, but telling me I might lie there and rot; which certainly must have been my fate had not an English soldier found me, who had, like myself, fallen into the hands of the enemy, but made his escape from them, and accidentally took shelter in my quarters, as I kept open house.

The poor fellow found me in a state of starvation, and took me upon his back (for I was quite help-less) to the village, and craved food for me from door to door ; but the inhuman Spaniards shut their doors in our faces, refusing me both shelter and food, at the same time they were baking bread for the French. However, my fellow sufferer, by good chance, found a dead horse, and he supplied me with this food and acorns, which at the time, I thought very dainty, believe me, and devoured when first given to me, in no small quantity, which nearly put an end to my sufferings.

I mention the following occurrence, in justice to the Spanish women; two girls, daughters of the prin-cipal person of the village, (a baker,) notwithstand-ing the threat of punishment to those who should relieve me, absolutely did, two or three times, bring me a little food, saved from their own meals.

In this miserable state I lay, when Colonel Gor-don,* one of Lord Wellington's aids-de-camp, found me, on his return to Rodrigo, from the French head quarters, where he had been with a flag of truce respecting General Sir Edward Paget, who had been made prisoner during the retreat.

He gave me a gold piece (three dollars) to buy bread with, and assisted my escape to Rodrigo, from

* Killed at Waterloo.

whence I was conveyed to the light division in a cart, a mere skeleton, and covered with all kinds of filth and vermin. Such, my dear brother, is the melancholy narrative of my unfortunate campaign; my appetite has been, ever since my escape from that unwholesome diet, most unmercifully ravenous; indeed dangerously so; for the surgeon was obliged at last, to forbid food being brought near me, or I should have brought on a fever from excessive eating. A dysentery still keeps me very weak, but I take a good deal of opium.

The ague still annoys me every other day, but the symptoms are not so violent as they used to be; in short, I have hopes now, that change of air and a little English beef, will soon restore me.

When I was missing after the retreat, I was given up as lost by the regiment, and all my things then with it, were sold; when rumours of my being still living reached head quarters, they were immediately collected again, and clean linen sent out to meet me. Colonel Barnard, (whose kindness I shall gratefully remember,) sent also several parties in various directions, in search of me, but they missed me, and I was brought in safe two or three days before their return.

I shall forward this by an officer, (being a more certain conveyance than by the country post,) who is returning to England by way of Oporto. I hope we shall be able to commence our journey about the middle of next month. I have lost most of my effects, one or two horses, and the £30 you sent me;

although I may think myself fortunate in escaping with my life, yet my pecuniary losses are great. However, I am content, hoping a few months' residence in my native air will bring me round again, and make me as stout as ever. The Spaniards were more inhuman in their treatment than the enemy.

I received one or two letters from you, while I lay ill at Salamanca, and I cannot describe what pleasure they gave me, although they lay in my bed a week or more, before I was able to understand from whom they came. I wished much to answer them, my dear brother, and more than once tried to do so, but found it impossible, nor had I any person to do it for me, for all were strangers about me, and I was delirious most part of the time.

It gave me the greatest pleasure to find that my dear parents were in such good health. My head at present is so much confused, that I fear you will find this a strange letter; indeed my brain, somehow or other, has been almost turned.

I hope we shall escape the banditti which infest Portugal, consisting of forty or fifty well armed men, mounted, chiefly deserters from the army; they have murdered several, and robbed a number of English officers, going to and from the army : there is one consolation for me, I have not much to lose at present, except my horses.

No news stirring here, except every thing is very scarce and dear, no money to be had; I have been obliged to sell several things, to enable me to purchase a few comforts. When at Salamanca, I was obliged to sell a few shirts and several other articles, to procure a chicken, for which I paid a dollar. In selling a pair of boots, the rascals would only give me a dollar and a half, knowing I was distressed for money: indeed I was miserably off, and several officers died in consequence of being destitute of cash to buy a few necessaries; I was nearly starved, like many others, and am only surprised to find myself living, and in a fair way of recovery.

Of the men who left England with us, not one-third are now living, and most of the finest fellows are gone; I have lost two servants.

The privations which the army suffered in the retreat from Burgos, were unusually severe; I saw many a brave fellow lying on the road, dying from fatigue, famine, and the inclemency of the weather. On one spot about one hundred English and Portuguese soldiers lay extended, after the retreat. One miserable instance, was, a soldier of the ninety-fifth, having marched as far as he was able, at last sunk from exhaustion, and crawled upon his hands and knees until he expired.

Lisbon, April the 16th. It is with the sincerest pleasure that I address you from this place. I arrived here a few days ago, after a very tedious journey through Portugal; and am happy to say, I find my health considerably improved, from the change of air, and exercise, so that I hope to take the field again sooner than I anticipated.

T——— and self, are so far on our way to England ; you may expect to see me soon, as I shall embark on board a transport, with two or three other officers of my regiment, who are returning home ; so you may look for me in three weeks or a month, at farthest. I hope, looking quite fat, in comparison to what I am now, for believe me, I am almost ashamed to appear in the streets at present, I make such a miserable show, and my clothes fit me like sacks. I long for every thing I see in the shape of eatables, but dare not indulge my appetite.

I enjoy vegetables much, and on my arrival at Lisbon, when some good food was put before me, I made such terrible meals, that I was afraid I should make myself ill again.

I have an offer of a passage home in a man-of-war, from the admiral commanding here, but prefer the society of my brother officers in the transport, as we are all convalescents : besides, we can fight our battles over again, and talk of the sufferings we have gone through,—this is a soldier's privilege.

We escaped the banditti, on our journey over the mountains, but an officer of the fourth dragoons was not so fortunate, who came down at the same time, he was robbed of his horses and baggage. I received a letter from the regiment yesterday ; every thing is quiet, no talk of commencing the campaign at present : the general opinion is, that scarcely any thing will be done this summer ; but I do not think so. It is also reported that 40,000 French have left Bur-

gos, with the whole of their baggage, for France.
This is in consequence of the disasters sustained by
Buonaparte in his Russian campaign.

Lord Wellington has sent down to Lisbon for
hunting saddles, bridles, &c.; this is also very likely,
as his lordship is desirous of keeping the soldiers of
his army amused, and on the *qui vive*.   But mark
me, he will soon hunt the French on the other side
of the Douro, when least expected.   This is all the
news from the light division.

Three regiments of dragoons are returning home
with us in the same convoy; they embark this day.
I sometimes, even now, feel so well, that I imagine
I could go through the fatigue of a campaign, but
the periodical attacks of ague upset my military
speculations; my legs also swell considerably towards evening, from debility.   My brother officers
are surprised at my presumption, in naming to them
that I had some intention of remaining in Lisbon for
the recovery of my health, and to hold myself in
readiness for the ensuing campaign. Captain T——
would not hear of it, and said it was a foolish point
of honour.   Farewell till we meet in England.

I remain,

Your truly affectionate brother,

ROBERT F——.

Lieut. ninety-fifth, riflemen.

CHAPTER XII.

From Lieutenant Robert F——'s arrival in England.—His embarkation for Spain in 1814.—Return to England, till his departure for Paris, in 1815.—His return the same year, until his death in Ireland, in 1828.

MY brother arrived in England on the 12th of May, 1813; he visited Staffordshire, and was for some time in extreme ill health; he was recommended by the deputy inspector of hospitals to go to Cheltenham, and found much benefit from the waters. A statement of his singular sufferings, accompanying his certificate of health, sent by myself, produced the following letter from Lieut.-General Sir Harry Calvert, Adjutant-general.

Horse Guards, August 2nd, 1813.

SIR,

I beg you will be assured that the delay of my reply to your letter of the 17th ult., has not proceeded from any want of consideration for your brother's situation, or feeling for his very extraordinary sufferings; on the contrary, I have taken an

opportunity of submitting his case to the Commander-in-chief, and to the Secretary of state, and I now
beg you will inform me by what means you conceive
his present situation can be relieved, or provision
can be best made for his comfort in future; and be
assured that I shall feel great pleasure in submitting
the same to the favourable consideration of the
Commander-in-chief.

I am, Sir,

Your very obedient servant,

HARRY CALVERT,

Adjutant-General.

Upon the receipt of the foregoing letter, my brother applied for promotion,—a company in a garrison, or second battalion in the line; refusing any
other reward for his services. He received the following letter from the Adjutant-General, written by
himself, a very unusual circumstance, and a mark
of great attention and respect.

Horse Guards, September 17th, 1813.

SIR,

In compliance with your brother's request, I
address to you my reply to his letter of the 11th instant, and I have much pleasure in assuring you,
that the Commander-in-chief has heard with much
interest the detail of your sufferings, and will be
happy in any opportunity of marking his sense of
your zeal, and the merits of your services, and will

recommend your promotion, as soon as he can do it with justice to other claims.

I enclose you a prolongation of your leave of absence, and I shall be extremely happy to hear of the re-establishment of your health.   I will transmit to your brother the letter which he desires may be returned, as soon as I receive it from the Commander-in-chief's office, where I placed it, in order to its being submitted to His Royal Highness's inspection.

I have the honour to be, Sir,

Your obedient humble servant,

HARRY CALVERT,*

Adjutant-General.

To Lieutenant F———,
    95th regiment.

Copy of a letter from Lieutenant-Colonel John, of the seventh battalion of the sixtieth regiment, (late Major, ninety-fifth regiment.)

Lip Hook, near Portsmouth,
September 8th, 1813.

MY DEAR F———,

You will, I fear, think me inattentive in not writing to you before ; believe me, I should have done so, but of late my time has been so occupied in matters concerned with my new corps, that I have had no time to attend to anything else.   I have considered your claims, and the Adjutant-General's let-

---

* Since Governor of Chelsea Hospital—now dead.

ter to you. Will it not be advisable, in the first instance, to see the Adjutant-General, and suggest to him your wishes ?

Command me in any way that I can be serviceable to you. To have you a captain in the battalion under my command, about to go to Canada, would be indeed, if it were practicable, highly gratifying to me. A company, I think, you are certain of succeeding to; and there are very few, believe me, that will rejoice more sincerely at any good fortune of yours, than I shall.

My future quarters, until we embark for North America, will be Newport, Isle of Wight, where I shall be delighted to see you; in the interim, I hope to be gratified by hearing from you. I am now on my way thither, and Mrs. J———, who is with me, desires her best compliments to you. Do come and see us.

Most faithfully,
My dear fellow, yours,
HENRY JOHN.

To Lieutenant F——— ,
  First battalion, 95th.

Lichfield,
November 1st, 1813.

My dear Brother,
      I returned from Cheltenham on Saturday last, after spending a month there. The journey has been expensive, but I do not regret the money,

though my funds are very low, from my losses in the Peninsula.

I am assured, by my medical attendant, that I may deduct fifteen years from my natural life, in consideration of my sufferings in Spain. God's will be done. I cannot think of asking for more leave, although I am not very stout, but no matter; under existing circumstances, I conceive it incompatible with the honourable feelings of an officer, whose regiment is to be actively employed during the winter; information of which I received from an officer of the light division, just before I left Cheltenham.

Do not believe that I undervalue life more than other people, but I do not wish to preserve it at the expense of my honour. You must not attribute this to bombast, (which I am afraid you will do,) but rather to a very different feeling—a sense of the duty I owe my regiment and brother officers.

I shall see you at all events before I leave England, and if we do not meet in town, I will come down to Colchester, the head quarters of your regiment. I shall want nearly £100, to fit out again, as I shall purchase two horses, for I never will run any unnecessary hazard for want of a good horse. My leave will expire in January next.

London, January 6th, 1814.—I met my friend F—— here, and we purpose leaving to-morrow; he wishes me to go down with him to Hythe, where he commands the depôt.

As I think the labours of Lord Wellington's army will be concluded in the approaching campaign, I shall join my regiment on service very soon. Two of my brother officers, who have recovered from their wounds, accompany me, once more to try the fickle goddess Fortune. I shall trouble you with a few little commissions about baggage, &c.

January 28th.—I reported myself officially at the Horse Guards on the 24th, and waited for orders. This morning I have attended again, and asked to see General Calvert; the man in waiting replied, "That the General was indisposed, and General Wynyard would transact business for him at the office." He requested me to put down my name, but I declined it, adding, I wished much to have seen General Calvert.

One of the attendants standing near, then said, that General C. would see no one there to-day, but Lieutenant F——, of the ninety-fifth. I immediately replied, " I am Lieutenant F——." I was desired to put my address on a card, and told that the General would see me presently. I was soon taken to his room, when he received me in the most polite and gentlemanly manner, and said, I must not think of going out immediately, as the weather was so severe, and that he would settle that point with His Royal Highness. I informed him that I was anxious to rejoin my regiment on service, as soon as the weather was milder, when the army would be on the move, as my health was much improved ; however, he would not hear of it. He inquired after you; I told him you were on leave.

February 17th.—I hope I shall go out to Canada with Colonel John. I have served and suffered enough as a subaltern, God knows! and I must say, the country has lost nothing by my services. To be sure there is one certainty, it cannot last for ever; this reconciles me in some measure to my lot, whether I fall in the field, or die on a bed, a captain or a subaltern.

February 26th.—I have again waited upon the Adjutant-General, urging my departure; but he would not consent until the 10th of March. I have received a letter this day from Colonel John, dated Guernsey, wherein he states that I should hear of him from Messrs. Cox and Greenwood; I went to their office, and learnt that he was expected in town every day. I had the pleasure of meeting with him the following day.

He recommended me strongly to write to the Adjutant-General again on the subject of my promotion, and has given me a letter, expressing his sentiments, advising my enclosing it to him; requesting permission, at the same time, to wait upon him before I left town.

The following is a copy of the Colonel's letter, which I have this morning enclosed to the Horse Guards.

Read's Hotel, Feb. 24th, 1814.

MY DEAR F——,

I am glad you have asked me to state my opinion of you as an officer, during the time you have been under my command in the third battalion of the ninety-fifth regiment, as it enables me to do that justice to your character, which your own conduct has on every occasion so well entitled you to. And I have no hesitation, but a very great satisfaction, in declaring to you, that I always found you a most attentive, active, and intelligent officer, and most zealous in the discharge of every duty.

And as a proof of what I express, nothing, I do assure you, would give me more pleasure, than to be so fortunate as to have you under my command. Wishing that you may soon get promotion, for I know of no one more fit to command a company,

I remain, my dear F——,

Yours very faithfully,

HENRY JOHN,

Lieut.-Col. 7th battalion, 60th foot.

To Lieutenant F——.

I shall write to him, when I have seen the Adjutant-General. The Colonel left town for Bristol this morning, expecting to meet Mrs. J——; he embarks with his regiment for Canada about the latter end of March. I met L—— this morning, he inquired after you.

March 3rd.—I enclosed Colonel John's letter, in one addressed to General Calvert, as follows :

London, Feb. 26th, 1814.

SIR,

As the period of my leaving England, to join my regiment on service, is drawing near, I am induced, (by the advice of my friends,) presuming on the kindness and indulgence you have hitherto manifested towards me, to address you once more on the subject of my promotion.

Lieutenant-Colonel John, my late commanding officer, with whom I met on my return to town, anxious for my future welfare, presented me with the enclosed, advising me to the step I have now taken, he himself not being sufficiently known to you, to make a personal application in my behalf; but recommending me, at the same time, to enclose his opinion of me as an officer, having served more immediately under his command in the rifle corps.

May I then, Sir, further presume on your goodness, to request your advice and assistance on this, to me, important occasion, before I quit this country, with leave to wait upon you, in the beginning of the week, previously to leaving town.

I have the honour to be, Sir,

Your very humble and obedient servant,

ROBERT F——,

First Lieut. 95th regiment.

To Lieut.-General Sir H. Calvert, &c. &c.

February 28th. As I had expressed my intention
of waiting upon the General this day; I repaired to
the Horse Guards, and sent up my name. I met
with a very kind reception from the Adjutant-General, who informed me that he had received my letter,
with its enclosure, that I might depend upon his assistance to forward my promotion, and that he would
immediately lay before the Duke of York my letter
and recommendation.

When I left him, I requested he would not lose
sight of me, in the event of my leaving England, he
assured me he would not; he then cordially shook
me by the hand, and I took my leave. He mentioned that the Duke applauded the zeal which I had so
often shown.

On the 11th of March my brother set off for
Portsmouth, as the transports had arrived to take out
the reinforcements for the south of France. About
one hundred riflemen had marched into that place
for embarkation, my brother taking the command, as
senior officer.

Portsmouth, March 15th, 1814.

My dear Brother,

I have just time to write a few lines before
we sail ; the wind is now fair, and the signal flying
for officers to repair on board. We are embarked
in the transport Henry, No. 13. Write to Layton
about my baggage ; I have arranged every thing
with him, if anything should prevent my return.

I have received a reply to my letter of the 8th instant, from the Horse Guards, with the Duke of York's permission to proceed on service, and his approval of my doing so. We are removed to the Thomas and Mary transport, No. 357.

Plymouth, March the 22nd. We have been obliged to put in here, from adverse winds, but it appears now more favourable. I command this detachment of riflemen, consisting of two lieutenants, part of the first battalion, and the band of the third battalion of the ninety-fifth. The enclosed, you will forward to Colonel John. In making my requests to you, I do not stand upon much ceremony. God bless you, my dear brother. I hope we shall meet again. Farewell.

Toulouse, May the 6th. We had a very unfavourable voyage out, but landed safe at Passages. The enclosed, my dear brother, I shall feel obliged to you to forward, it is the fulfilment of a promise. Our march across the Pyrenees was fatiguing, but I would not have missed it for a good deal; the scenery was magnificent and sublime; I cannot express my admiration in words. Although it is now three weeks since we passed over the mountains, they are still in sight. I brought a serious charge with me up to Toulouse, sixty mules laden with specie. I felt much anxiety for its safety during the march, however, I delivered it safe to the paymaster-general.

Toulouse is a very ancient city; many of the nobles reside here, and the inhabitants, generally, are

favourable to the Bourbons. It is fortified with an
old rampart, flanked by round towers, and is capable of making an obstinate defence, being surrounded on three sides by the canal of Languedoc, uniting
the two seas, and by the river Garonne.

It was under the walls of this city that the Duke
of Dalmatia resolved to make a great effort; he established batteries, and entrenchments under them,
and covered the whole by his artillery and musketry
from the rampart, thereby making it a formidable
tête de pont.

He also secured the bridges over the canal by
similar means, covering them by the French artillery,
and lines of musketry from the old walls.

On the neighbouring heights, Soult established a
chain of redoubts, adding strongly indented lines of
entrenchments. He strengthened these by a powerful chain of fortifications, mounted by his artillery.
In this position the Duke of Wellington determined
attack him.

It has since appeared, that Soult knew of the abdi-
cation of Buonaparte, at the time, but suppressed the
intelligence, so that Lord Wellington remained in
ignorance of the allied armies being in possession of
Paris.

A most brilliant attack was made by Marshal Beresford along the heights, storming the several fortified places, trenches, and redoubts in succession as
he advanced, under a galling and destructive fire of
cannon and musketry, to the astonishment of the

French; in short, he traversed with his division the entire range, carrying the whole before him, from one extremity to the other ; and to sum up, this sanguinary battle, fought under the walls of Toulouse, to the terror and dreadful suspense of the inhabitants, was won, the French being unable to check the victorious career of the Duke of Wellington ; finally the British army, to their great joy, entered Toulouse, and hoisted the white flag of the Bourbons.

Marshal Soult sent in his adhesion to the new Government, desiring a suspension of hostilities. This glorious action was the last fought in the campaign of 1814.

We expect soon to be in England ; our men are having new clothing made. I am going in a day or two to Milhaud, several days' ride on the Paris road, and intend returning by Montabaun, through the forest, to Toulouse. We find the French courteous ; the country around this place is very beautiful ; the Garonne runs under my window.

A grand fête was given to us a few days ago, by the Marquis de Pompignon ; the Duke of Wellington gives a ball to-night, and the Duke of Dalmatia is invited. The fête at the Marquis de Pompignon's was very pleasant; we assembled in his garden about dusk, where two batteries were erected, occupied by French ladies. We stormed them, they were well defended by our fair foes, but at last they were obliged to surrender at discretion.

Just before the commencement of the attack, one of the ladies deserted to us, and led us to the most assailable point. Afterwards we had a play, ball, and the whole concluded with an elegant supper. The little deserter took a leading part in every thing during the evening.

The French people had been taught by their soldiers, that the English were cruel, that we should plunder and maltreat them. We expect orders to march to Bourdeaux, in order to embark for England.

Plymouth, July the 25th. We arrived here in the Dublin, and Queen Charlotte, from Bourdeaux. This city hoisted the white flag on the 12th of March ; the authorities met Marshal Beresford, accompanied by the Duc d'Angouleme, with the greatest enthusiasm. It is a fine place, built in the form of a bow, and the Garonne makes the string. We were reviewed here before our embarkation for England.

I shall send this letter by Sir John R——, who is going by the mail, and as soon as I can learn our future destination, I purpose going up myself. We rather expect to cross the Atlantic, for American service. Our first and second battalions are gone to Portsmouth, where they are at present halted.

August the 4th. I am sorry to say, my dear brother, that the blessings of peace have not reached us, for instead of marching into the interior, we are ordered to hold ourselves in readiness to embark for America. I should have been quite content to have remained in England, had it been so ordered, but such is the uncertainty of a soldier's life.

I do not belong to the third battalion, for since my promotion, I was attached to the first, but having preferred serving with the third, I cannot now leave it, since it has been ordered on service. Five companies only are under orders, consequently, our right wing stands first for duty; the other two battalions are on their march into Kent; I hope the American business will be a short one.

The forty-third light infantry joins 'us; its second battalion is on the march to join the first, and after the finest men are selected the remainder is to be reduced. We have completed the wing to 500 men. One of our officers who knows America well, says, campaigning will be worse than in Spain; however, I hope they will not forget my promotion at home, if they indulge me with this trip, to compensate me for eleven years' service, and the expense of fitting out for this American campaign.

Plymouth, August the 16th. An order has been received from the Horse Guards, by the commanding officer of the third battalion, to instruct me to proceed to Shorncliff, to join the first battalion, to which I belong. I am reluctant to quit the third, it being under orders for service; had it rested with myself, I should not hesitate a moment in the choice; but as it appears an act of the Adjutant-General's, I must obey; however it is correct to be on the right side; the following is the notification.

Horse Guards,
8th of August 1814.

SIR,

I am directed to acquaint you, that his Royal Highness, the Commander-in-chief, approves of your instructing Lieutenant F—— to proceed to Shorncliff, for the purpose of joining the first battalion, ninety-fifth regiment, to which he belongs.

I have the honour to be, Sir,
Your obedient servant,
HARRY CALVERT.
Adj.-Gen.

Officer commanding third batt. ninety-fifth regt.
    Plymouth.

The forty-third, ninety-third, and ninety-fifth, were reviewed this morning, and very flattering encomiums were personally passed by the General, on the warlike appearance of the troops.

London, August the 30th. Our new commanding officer, Major Mitchel, not arriving before the latter end of the week, I could not set out sooner ; with reluctance, I parted from my old companions in arms, who were preparing for embarkation.

The Major gave me orders to proceed to Shorncliff, to join the first battalion, being returned to the War Office, "on my way to join." Major B—— is also transferred from the third, to the first ; we travelled up together. I asked B—— if I could be allowed to join the third, if I wished it, on service ?

He replied, Certainly not, without an imperative order.

September 7th.—I have been to see an old brother officer, who resides at Old Brompton. I have just met with Major L. G——, and we have agreed to go together, understanding that the first battalion, ninety-fifth, is on its march to Dover. This move will delay our journey a short time, until the regiment is settled in barracks, therefore we shall not join until the 24th. With respect to my losses in the Peninsula, we will talk over the matter when we meet.

Dover Heights, November 6th.—As things are now quiet, and little to do, I purpose paying a visit to you in Northamptonshire, that is, if we are not ordered to America. An order has just arrived for part of our regiment to embark for Flanders to-morrow morning, but I am not included. I have got leave, and shall spend part of my time with you at Peterborough, and the remainder at Lichfield. I have leave until the 10th of March.

Shorncliff, March 12th, 1815.—I arrived here on the expiration of my leave. We have received accounts from New Orleans : our regiment has suffered severely. Major-General the Hon. Sir Edward Pakenham, (whom you remember in command of the sixty-fourth regiment, in Barbadoes,) is killed. Major-General Gibbs is dead of his wounds. The total killed and wounded about 2000.

Rear-Admiral Malcolm, (our dear brother John's

kind commander,) superintended the debarkation. His talents are highly spoken of, as to his prompt and skilful manner of arrangement. We are daily expecting our men from America; out of the 500, about 200 effective remain.

April 10th.—The Gazettes from Canada speak highly of my gallant friend, Colonel John. The following notice of him is made by Lieutenant-General Sir J. C. Sherbroke, K. B. from the despatches of September 18, 1814. " Castine, at the entrance of the Penobscot.—The enterprise and intrepidity manifested by Colonel John, and the discipline and gallantry displayed by the troops under him, reflect great honour on them, and demand my warmest acknowledgments." And again, from Captain Barrie, of the Dragon, to Vice-Admiral Sir Alexander Cochrane, K. B., September 3rd, 1814. " I cannot close my report without expressing my highest admiration of the very gallant conduct of Colonel John, the officers and soldiers under his command; for, exclusive of the battery above named, they had difficulties to contend with on their left, which did not fall under my observation, as the enemy's fieldpieces in that direction were masked. The utmost cordiality existed between the two services; and I shall ever feel obliged to Colonel John, for his ready co-operation in every thing that was proposed."

The Colonel's services in America were brilliant, and I lament that it was not my good fortune to serve under him. He was an inestimable officer.

Shorncliff, May 15.—I had promised myself the pleasure of meeting you in town, my dear brother, on Tuesday; but the arrival of General Stewart, and our half-yearly inspection, have intervened. The General has been looking at his regiment this morning; he kindly shook hands with me, and inquired after you.

Our men have landed from America, and are waiting for orders at Portsmouth to join us here. I am again attached to the third battalion. The General is looking very ill, and seems much out of spirits; he remains with us this week. The depôts of the first and second battalions have just marched in here from Dover.

Shorncliff, May 21.—The Hon. Lieutenant-General Sir William Stewart dined with us on Friday, and on the following morning took his departure for London. After he left the dinner table, I took the opportunity of enclosing for his perusal my correspondence with the Horse Guards. He returned with the papers the following note.

Friday evening, 19th May, 1815.

I return you, my dear Sir, the papers you sent for my perusal, and I shall be pleased by aiding your views, whenever in my power and with prospect of success. I should like to have read the statement of your sufferings in Spain, apparently alluded.to. My residence in London is, 4, Hereford Street. If you send me the papers, let not the letter,

&c. weigh more than an ounce, in one or more covers.

Yours faithfully,

WILLIAM STEWART.

To Lieutenant F——,
Ninety-fifth regiment.

As you, my dear brother, have the account of my unfortunate campaign, I will thank you to send it up to the General, according to his request. I mentioned your present pursuits to him. He is an excellent man; he has presented the soldiers' children with five guineas, and done many other charitable acts; given the mess fund twenty pounds and a handsome silver snuff box. One of our serjeants owed him ten pounds, which he has not been able to repay; the General has forgiven him the debt, and has left a memorandum with me, certifying to the Quarter-Master that he had done so, to be given him on his return from America.

Copy of a letter from Lieutenant-General the Hon. Sir William Stewart, in answer to one enclosing my brother's narrative.

London, No. 4, Hereford Street,
June 2, 1815.

DEAR SIR,

I have to thank you very much for the interesting letter and narrative, herewith returned, which, having heard much relative thereto, when in Portugal, in 1813, I was anxious to peruse. Great as was the sacrifice that your brother made to the marine service, by entering the army, and small as has been his reward, comparatively with his merit, both you and he are too well aware of the difficulties which stand in the way of promotion without purchase, to be impatient as to the result of even the favourable notice that he received at the Horse Guards, and from the Adjutant-General personally, and of which he did me the honour to make communication, when I was lately at Shorncliff.

He or you will of course retain these interesting documents, and produce them in support of his advancement, whenever the opportunity shall suit. If on such occasion I can be of use, I shall be so with pleasure; but at this moment the list of candidates from the half-pay is so great, that the oldest and most meritorious subalterns will, I apprehend, have some delay to encounter. I thank you for your prospectus, and enclosed paper relative to your work. I shall take an early opportunity of calling upon your bookseller, in Pall Mall, to look at your Johnsoniana.

I have the honour to be,

Yours faithfully,

WILLIAM STEWART.*

* This was the last letter I received from my much honoured patron and friend, the gallant and illustrious General, the Hon. Sir William Stewart. In the course of his active service, he had received six wounds and four contusions; since dead.

Shorncliff, June 29th, 1815.—I should have written sooner to you, my dear brother, but since the battle of Waterloo, on the 18th, we have been hourly in expectation of orders to embark for France. We have eight companies of the third battalion here, and only two were at Waterloo. We should have been there too, but have been waiting for our new arms.

July 9th.—Our orders are arrived to march to Dover, and embark immediately for France; to take every effective man we can muster; and are all hurry and bustle in consequence. Thirty-five horses are just embarked. The men are now falling in. God bless you all. Farewell.

Paris, August 2nd.—We had a rapid march through the country, following the route of the Prussians, who have amply repaid the French for their conduct at Berlin. Our appearance created some alarm, as we were taken for a detachment of the Prussian army, on account of our dark uniforms. The inhabitants fled from us with horror, until we assured them we were English, on our march to Paris.

We were occasionally quartered at some of the chateaus, and found some of the ornamental rooms often defaced by the spoliation of the Prussians, who exercised their men in the drawing rooms, broke in pieces the furniture, and disfigured the walls, &c.

Paris was taken possession of on the 7th July,

within three weeks after the glorious victory at Waterloo, by 50,000 of the allied troops, British and Prussians, who entered the capital of France, defiling along the Boulevards and the alleys of the Champs Elysees. What a different feeling pervaded the allies, and the French people, from the joyous procession of 1814. Paris was occupied as a conquered city; the conquerors marched in with all the stern appearance of war ; guns loaded, matches lighted, and the city was garrisoned as a captured place, with suspicion of an insurrectionary movement. The heights of Montmartre were taken possession of by the English, also the bridges, squares, and principal barriers, as military posts; loaded cannon were planted on the Pont Neuf and Pont Royal, attended by soldiers with lighted matches. Such was the state of affairs when we arrived, and were stationed at the barriers.

We continued on duty here, when, on the 20th September, commenced the dispersion of the Museum, &c. at the Louvre, of the paintings, statues, &c. which were taken away, in order to be restored to those countries from which they had been plundered.

The Transfiguration, by Raphael, I shall never recollect but with the most enthusiastic admiration. I have sat many hours at a time before this sublime picture. Such was the effect produced upon the Cossacks, that they appeared overcome with awe,

s 2

gazing upon it with astonishment, their long spears in their hands.

One day I was gazing attentively on this matchless production, deeply absorbed in contemplation of its awful sublimity, when I was tapped upon the shoulder by Prince Schwartzenburgh, who did me the honour to enter into conversation on its merits.

The allied troops assembled round Paris, amounted to near 800,000 men, at free quarters, and heavy requisitions were imposed from time to time for their clothing and subsistence. Such an immense army collected to one focus was never before seen in Europe.

How little did France calculate, when she oppressed her neighbours, that she should have been twice invaded, and at last occupied as a conquered country! The Prussians, under the Prince Marshal Blucher, removed the pictures belonging to their sovereign, without ceremony. We go on tolerably quiet, observing the strictest discipline.

November 15th.—The final arrangement respecting the future quarters of the allies, is now completed: the allied forces of Austria, Russia, Prussia, &c. are to occupy the country around Paris; our second battalion, with its division, is gone to Versailles; the first battalion, and its division, have moved near to St. Germain; and the third battalion, with its division, occupies Paris, with the brigade of Guards. We are stationed at all the principal en-

trances into the city, denominated Barriers. The
remainder of the British army is quartered in the
country around the capital, not being more than one
day's march distant from it.

All these precautions are necessary, in case of
alarm, for the country is very unsettled at present.
The strictest discipline is observed. I am at this
instant on duty at one of the barriers, and compelled to suspend my letter for a few minutes, to receive Louis XVIII., who is passing my post.

We have regular places of assembly, in case of
alarm, for each regiment, and our duties are very
strictly inspected. I hope that our battalion will
soon be in England, as we expect our orders daily.

Shorncliff, December 29th.—Our orders were very
sudden; we received them late in the afternoon on
the 2nd, and on the 3rd December, at daylight, we
commenced our march from Paris to Boulogne,
where we embarked, and landed at Dover a few
days ago. We had a very cold march through
France to Boulogne; some part of the way through
deep snow; some days lodging in palaces, and on
others in cabins. I addressed a letter to my brother,
at his recruiting station, but have been since informed he is in Ireland with his regiment. Our
future destination will be Dublin.

The Author suspends his brother's papers, to give
a brief account of himself.

January 20, 1816.—Having taken the recruiting

parties over to Dublin, I remained on duty with my
regiment for some time at the Castle.   In February
I was ordered to Swords, to relieve a party of the
King's County militia, and to assist the magistrates,
where I continued until the middle of April.   I was
then relieved at my quarters, by Lieutenant Bruce,
of the third battalion, ninety-fifth regiment, who
informed me that my brother had embarked from
England, in charge of the horses of the regiment,
but had not yet arrived.

I marched my party into Dublin, and, under the
archway of the Palatine Square, I had the singular
happiness of shaking by the hand my dear brother,
who had landed that day at the Pigeon House.   We
passed several days together, when I embarked with
my regiment for England, and was disembodied on
April 24th, 1816.

My brother continued with the rifle brigade in
Dublin, on duty, and being an amateur artist, he
was admitted an honorary member of the Dublin
Academy, and painted several pictures, under the
auspices of Mr. W——.   " The Conversion of Saul;"
" Charles I. from Vandyke," which he presented to
Lord R——.   He painted also the " Holy Trinity,"
and several others.   Mr. W—— painted my brother's
picture.

The following melancholy case of hydrophobia
occurred in the regiment, and is related by my
brother as follows.

Royal Barracks, Dublin,
15th August, 1816.

On Sunday the 14th instant I sent an account of a melancholy event, which happened to an excellent and much lamented young man and brother officer, who died of hydrophobia a few days ago; I add what I witnessed myself, together with what I learnt from my poor friend, who is, alas! now no more.

About three months ago, a large French dog, belonging to one of the officers, was observed to grow uncommonly surly, and attempted to bite at every dog he met in the streets; this change of temper in the animal was attributed by his master, (who was very fond of him,) to his having eaten a quantity of meat, which had been given to him, highly seasoned with pepper, &c. However, towards the evening of the day on which the change in the animal was perceived, he became at intervals quite outrageous, and bit his master, and two more officers who happened to be in the room; notwithstanding, his master was inclined to think it was done more in rude play than any thing else, consequently no measure was taken to secure him.

That evening I saw the dog, and thought him uncommonly unruffled; when I attempted to caress him, and was patting him on the back, he turned at me, and savagely growled, although he used to know me well. The next day he was more violent, and furiously bit at several dogs who crossed his way; still, unfortunately, no measure was taken to secure him, his master supposing nothing was the matter with him.

On the evening of the second day, the dog was lying in his master's room, perfectly tranquil, when this unfortunate young man (who has fallen the victim) entered; he remained in it some time before the dog took any notice of him; however, he suddenly made a spring at him, seized him by the shoulder, and pulled him to the ground, and tore the arm down to the shoulder, and was with difficulty taken off him.

A serjeant of the regiment happened to enter the room on duty, about this time; the dog seized him by the leg, and tore away a considerable portion of flesh ; he bit also two soldiers, one by the nose and the other on the hand. Still the animal was suffered to be at large, and even slept in his master's room, by his bedside, and licked his face repeatedly. The following morning the master of the dog began to feel some alarm, and asked me to go with him to look at him. I advised him to have him shot; he agreed. As we were going to the spot where he lay, he bolted up, snapping at every thing which came in his way. He passed close by me; I called him, but he did not notice me.

He ran through the streets of Dublin; bit a number of dogs and a child ; he attempted to seize a man, who fortunately had a hammer in his hand, with which he struck him on the head and killed him.

The tongue of the dog was immediately cut out, upon the spot, by a physician, and on examination pronounced the animal to have been in an advanced stage of hydrophobia.

None of the officers or soldiers who had been bitten, knew the decision of the physician, nor did they know of any ill effects having arisen to those who had been bitten. However, the child died; and three dogs which had been bitten died in about six weeks, exhibiting symptoms of hydrophobia.

All this was kept secret, therefore no cause of alarm from report could have excited hydrophobic feelings in the unfortunate young man who has fallen a sacrifice; on the contrary, he was in high spirits, and applied for leave of absence to go and see his friends in Worcestershire, as he had some intentions of being married. He obtained leave, thinking it might divert his attention, and he left us with the same flow of spirits. During his absence all was forgotten; and those remaining who had suffered, (though not quite so severely,) recovered their cheerful habits.

The period of leave granted to my poor friend having expired, he set out from his father's house a few days ago, in perfect health, to rejoin his regiment. (This he told me a few hours before he died.) When he got to Birmingham, he said he had a curious taste in his mouth, which made him not relish his breakfast as usual. However, it gave him no alarm, nor did he again think of it till he got to Shrewsbury, when he found he had a great disrelish to both eatables and drinkables when put before him, although he felt an inclination to eat and drink when not before him.

He could not account for this, but observed he felt no alarm, until he called for porter, feeling thirsty. When it was brought, he put it to his mouth, but the moment he took a mouthful, he dashed the glass from his lips, and spit the porter over the table, and I believe the passengers rose up and said he was mad. This extraordinary feeling, of not being able to eat and drink, though he wished to do so, caused him some uneasiness, though he was willing to believe it was the effect of a sore throat, and comforted himself under this idea.

He proceeded by the coach to Holyhead, ruminating what could be the cause of this sensation, when the coach passed a small lake of water, the surface of which being ruffled by the wind, he immediately shuddered at the sight, and with a kind of horror he could not describe, hid his face with his hands;—for the first time, the dreadful idea of hydrophobia struck him.

When he arrived at Holyhead, he wished to wash before dinner, and called for water; when it was brought to him, and in the act of putting it towards his face, he screamed violently, threw the water about the room, and was convulsed for some time; the servant left the room alarmed. He then tried to clean his teeth, but could not get the brush into his mouth, on account of the water remaining upon it.

The packet by this time was ready to sail, and he embarked.

Poor fellow! while he was relating his sad tale to me, we were sitting together by the fireside, he having just landed from Holyhead, which place he sailed from the night before, consequently this was the third day only since his attack at Shrewsbury. He had then been on shore about two hours, and had ordered a coach, and drove up to the royal barracks.

Before he began to tell me, on his arrival, of the symptoms he had experienced on his journey, he greeted me on our first meeting, with " How are you, my dear fellow? Here I am at last returned, but I fear with hydrophobia!" I affected to laugh at it, but was much shocked, and replied, it could only be imaginary; he said, it could not be so, for he thought he should have died coming on shore in the boat; he was so much affected at the sight of the water, that they were obliged to cover him, in order that he might not see it. He also observed, that if he had remained on board one day longer, he felt convinced that he should have died mad.

I was still inclined to think there might be a good deal of imagination in my friend, and endeavoured to persuade him to believe so; although I cannot describe the poignancy of my feelings, at hearing him relate what he suffered at intervals, since he left Shrewsbury.

In the course of our conversation, some dogs

began to bark in the barrack yard; he sprang up
suddenly from his chair, looking over my shoulder,
and said in a hurried manner, " Dogs !" If I were
to live a thousand years, I should never forget that
moment; something struck me so forcibly that the
poor sufferer would die, that I was afraid to meet
his eyes, fearing he might discern signs of alarm in
me, from emotion.

He was in the act of peeling an orange, which we
had persuaded him to try to eat, as he had taken
nothing since he rejected the porter at Shrewsbury.
When he had taken off the rind, he put a small piece
into his mouth; but as soon as he felt the liquid, he
became greatly convulsed, spit out the orange, and
gave an inward scream. When he recovered himself, he burst into a fit of laughter, and said,
" There! was not that like the bark of a dog?"

A physician arrived soon after, who is eminent in
Dublin. As soon as he entered the room, the poor
fellow apologized to him for having given him the
trouble to come, as he thought he had symptoms of
hydrophobia, but believed it was only the effect of a
sore throat, therefore would give him no further
trouble. He appeared to catch at any thing which
might give hopes of life.

We were very anxious to learn the decision of the
physician, on his leaving the room; upon inquiry,
he pronounced his death, to be inevitable. It is unnecessary to describe the state of our minds, on receiving this melancholy news—to know that our

brother officer, with whom we were conversing, to all external appearance, in perfect health, and apparent spirits, was to be numbered with the dead in a few hours, was deeply distressing.

The doctor added, that he was in an advanced stage of hydrophobia, that bleeding him copiously, in order that he might die easy, was the only thing that could now be done for him. I remained with him some time, conversing about various things, (though completely forced on my part,) as his spirits remained good. On leaving him, I asked him when he intended to dine at the mess, he replied, he could not dine with us that day, but he thought he should be able to do so, in a day or two, when his sore throat was better.

After he was bled he felt relieved, thought he should sleep well, and hoped to be able to drink water, by the next morning. Some time after, in the course of the evening, he appeared at intervals, rather wild and confused, and told an officer to get out of his way, or he would bite him. Afterwards, he became more tranquil, and sent his compliments to one of the married ladies of the regiment, for a prayer book, but begged it might not be mentioned, or he should be laughed at.

About midnight he became very violent, so that three men could scarcely hold him; he afterwards recovered a little, and fell into a kind of slumber, which was disturbed by his springing up now and then, and crying out, "Do you hear the dogs?"—in a quick and hurried voice; he also, imagined at times, that he barked like a dog,

He requested he might be left alone, about one o'clock in the morning, his servant, only, remaining in the room, when in about ten minutes, he looked up at the man, quite calm and collected, and said, " he regretted that his mother, and sisters were not with him ;"—he then prayed a short time, turned himself round, burying his face in the pillow,—and expired without a groan.———Such was the melancholy end of one of the finest young men in His Majesty's service.

This mournful catastrophe, has thrown a gloom over the garrison of Dublin. His remains were interred the day before yesterday, with military honours, attended by the rifle brigade, and every officer in and about the garrison. The general officers attended, and all wore military mourning.

There remain three officers, and three soldiers of the regiment who were bitten; their spirits are much depressed on this occasion. It is intended to erect a monument to the memory of our lamented brother officer.

My brother paid me a visit at Peterborough, from Ireland, at the beginning of 1817. Afterwards proceeded into Staffordshire; where I joined him. We parted, alas !—for the last time, on his return to that country; he had given up all chance of promotion. The great reduction in the army, consequently includ-

ing many officers, rendered every application hope-
less and unavailing; he felt his disappointment, but
there was no help for it. He rejoined his regiment
on the 10th of March, and continued on duty, in
Dublin, till the summer of 1818. As the following
extract will show.

"Royal Barracks, Dublin, July the 19th, 1818.
We are now expecting a change of quarters, and
some of the regiments are now on the move. It is
intended by the Commander of the forces, that all
corps shall have completed their march to their new
stations, by the middle of July. We are ordered to
the King's County."

My brother continued with the third battalion of
the rifle brigade, until the commencement of 1819,
when it was disbanded, and the officers placed on
half-pay. His case was considered worthy of notice,
and was under consideration at the Horse Guards;
but nothing was done. I was at this time in London,
and had a personal interview with the Adjutant-
General, who exerted his interest in my brother's behalf; but from the great number of claimants, whose
services were equally meritorious, he was finally
obliged to retire upon a lieutenant's half-pay. He
made no complaints; but his disappointment was
severely felt. About this time, he married the Hon.
Mrs. ———, and settled in Ireland.

Here he received an appointment, the command
of the constabulary force in his neighbourhood; the

following extracts from his letters, will point out the
nature of his official occupation.

P——— , January the 11th, 1825.   A happy new
year to yourself, my dear sister, and all your family ;
and may you live to enjoy many succeeding ones.
Some of my old Spanish hardships, at least, the re-
sults, have rebelled greatly against me, to the detri-
ment of my health.   I have had some very serious
liver attacks ; they became so frequent, that I was
obliged to call in the first advice in Ireland.   I
have met with the most unbounded kindness from
Lord ———.

This country has been in a state of alarm, at the
approach of 1825.   It was predicted that the Pro-
testants were to be massacred ; but thanks be to
God, we are still living, and, as my dear father used
to say, have been for many years.   The poorer clas-
ses, I allow, might be better off, but the activity of
the police, prevents many wanton disorders, which
would increase their distress.

I travel sometimes through my district, with no
one but my own servant, at all hours of the night;
I most frequently go without police cavalry, and am
never molested.

February the 3rd, 1827.   My duty is now severe,
as the country is disturbed.   England has its advantages over Ireland, peace and obedience to the laws,
which carry along with them, prosperity, comfort,
and security ; these, I am sorry to say, we know little

about.   However, we get accustomed to these things
from habit and daily example.

Broken heads are as common here on a market
day, (indeed, I may say, on all other days,) as ginger-
bread stalls at a country fair in England; and were
it not for the military police, established in this
country, it would scarcely be possible to live in it:
perhaps, I should not say this, belonging to that establishment, but it is a fact, well known from dearly-
bought experience; if I were to enumerate the various outrages, you would be surprised.

January the 27th, 1828.   I have been very ill
indeed, but am rather better.   I do not see, or even
hear of, so fine a couple as our dear parents are;*
such are not to be found in this country.

I have been a great martyr to bilious attacks, however, I trust time and patience will do much for me,
with regular hours and living; but unfortunately, I
cannot command the former, as I am still liable to
be called out, at all seasons, both day and night.
This country is destroyed by religious dissensions
and party spirit.

The short time I was at the sea last summer, was
of service to me, but I have had a return, though not
so severe.   I had not the full benefit of the salt
water, as I was called to my duty one month earlier
than I expected, in consequence of several serious
outrages having occurred, during my absence, in my

* Their united ages, 164 years.

T

district. About six weeks ago I had a severe fit of illness, in the county of Tipperary; being summoned on duty, I got a sad wetting, and imprudently sat in my wet clothes, which brought on a violent fever; luckily I was near the place of my brother-in-law, —————, who had every care and attention shown me; I was excessively ill for a time, but fortunately recovered. The next time you hear from me will probably be from the county of Kilkenny, where I expect to be removed, in a general change of constabulary throughout Ireland.

This was the last letter my brother addressed to England; he died suddenly, on the 28th of April, 1828, in the forty-fourth year of his age. The following notice of his decease is from the Dublin Warder, of May 10th.

" At P——, on the 28th ult., of paralysis, Robert F——, Esq. late of the rifle brigade, and until his death, in the command of the constabulary force of that neighbourhood; all the duties of which he discharged with zeal, forbearance, and efficiency. In private life, society has to mourn the loss of the affectionate friend, as well as the accomplished gentleman; gifted pre-eminently by nature, and highly cultivated by education, he won with facility the esteem of all that approached him, but more by the urbanity and modesty of his nature, than by the aid of those accomplishments, which so justly distinguished him in the numerous circle in which he moved. He has left behind a disconsolate widow, and five small children, to lament, in common with a large circle of friends, his untimely and irreparable loss."

FINIS.

PRINTED BY J. MASTERS, ALDERSGATE STREET.

For a free catalogue, telephone

Spellmount Publishers on

01580 893730

or write to

The Old Rectory

Staplehurst

Kent TN12 0AZ

United Kingdom

(Facsimile 01580 893731)

(e-mail enquiries@spellmount.com)

(Website www.spellmount.com)